CW00394650

PUBLISHED 13 December 2019

Day after General Election

www.TheSmartPlan.co.uk

www.linkedin.com/company/thesmartplan

Twitter   @plansmartly

Email   info@thesmartplan.co.uk

Printed via Amazon

First edition 2019

ISBN 9781671991651

Independently published

CLARE BRANTON
For David Branton
who taught me to work hard and keep learning
And to all the great people who I have been privileged to learn from Madeleine Cox,
Francine Cole, Babs Davies, Noah Evans, Eric Simpson, Nigel Kirkup, James Bunt,
Joe Waterton, Mark Hope, Pat Foran, Louise King, Tim Clarke, Camila Kill,
Simon Warbey, Sherwin Jarvand, Colin Davey, George Meudell, Peter Ashton,
Julian Coghlan, Jacqui Rigby, Paul Flynn and Glenn Benson.

NICK
For Henry Davies
And all the many talented people I have worked with. Too many to name but specifically Dr Sue
Waldock, Paul Armitage and my HR colleagues from the Rank group and Betclic – many of whom
I continue to enjoy and share learning experiences with Carolyn Lambourne, Rob Hamblin,
Veronique Giraudon and the island of Malta.

ERICA
For Clare, Simon, Jessica, Leon
and to all creative friends, family, past, present and future.

About us

Nick and I met at the John Lewis Partnership in the late 1980s where best practice was in the DNA. We moved on, but have stayed firm friends.

Earlier this year as we were talking about Project BREXIT we were struck by how much best practice was being ignored, and also how the challenges mirrored some of those we had experienced ourselves.

We have always been passionate about practical and emotionally engaging learning experiences. An experience that will really mean something. So learning from Project BREXIT seemed the perfect way to share our combined 50+ years of insights .

Erica has been able to breath life into our thoughts with her illustrations.

We hope you enjoy the book as much as we have enjoyed making it.

Clare
Dec 2019

CLARE BRANTON

Since leaving John Lewis I have worked with marketeers at GUINNESS UDV and MICROSOFT, with curators and conservators at the VICTORIA & ALBERT MUSEUM, digital innovators at the TUI GROUP and more beside!
Every experience has taught me something. Every experience has been valued.
I love sharing my learnings and this book has been a great way of doing that. It is inspired by my love of history, current affairs, football and popular culture. I am equally at home watching David Olusoga, Question Time, Match of the Day, Star Wars or Strictly Come Dancing.

NICK DAVIES

I have spent nearly 30 years in Human Resources within both Retail and Digital businesses, mostly in the gaming sector with the RANK GROUP and BETCLIC. Having worked through a period of immense business, social and technological change, I jumped at the chance of 'downloading' some of my learning.
You can either resist change, in which case it will drag you along by the heels whether you like it or not, or choose to move with it and play your part in the game.
In a world of systems, software, AI, Augmented Reality and data science you need to know that evolution gave priority to the part of the brain that deals with emotions and feeling rather than logic.
So let your project be driven by this rather than new software or spreadsheets !

ERICA WARBEY

Since forever ... always sketching from flora to fauna, architecture to politicians...
Throughout degrees, data analysis reporting, qualifying to teach... to collaborative creative projects from school trips sketching London to illustrating books!

THE SMART PLAN
How to enjoy this book

Intro
How to plan smartly

SMART
Specific
Measurable
Achievable
Relevant
Timeframed

Themes
A-Z themes to help you deliver your project, and evaluate how well Project BREXIT has done.

A-Z

Best Practice
Acknowledged best practice and insights from making change happen in the real world.

Focus on
Background information for a key concept or technique.

Quotes
Commentary from history, sport, politics and the world of celebrity.

What Brexit Did
Key BREXIT Learning Points

Examples of what happened to project BREXIT

THE SMART PLAN
Contents

Intro

Themes

NATIONAL AUDIT OFFICE
Website DEC 2019
"Departments have achieved a lot so far, but exiting the EU is no ordinary task. Departments have had to prepare for multiple potential outcomes, with shifting timetables and ongoing uncertainty. It is a task that has little or no historical precedent"

THE UK & THE EU
MARCH 2019
Nathalie Loiseau, France's EU minister names her cat BREXIT

"he meows loudly to be let out but won't go through the door"

BREXIT A TO Z
Thousands of sites available to Google – and that's just the ones in English.
Also …
Polish, German, French sites

And … even …
Brexit A to Z of lies !

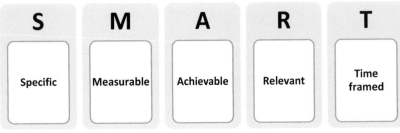

S	M	A	R	T
Specific	Measurable	Achievable	Relevant	Time framed

The widely used acronym to help drive success by setting clearly defined objectives

Plan Smartly

What is a project?   A project is a collection of activities focused on achieving a result. The result will add value for you and your customers, and will use agreed resources, timeframe and budget.

Projects absorb people, time and money.   Being SMART helps you to use these resources wisely and effectively.

Each of the 5 SMART views help you make clear and targeted objectives to describe your project.

So whether your project is solving a problem or making the most of an opportunity, a SMART Plan gives you the best chance of success.

WHAT BREXIT DID

BREXIT has not felt like a project. It has become a series of repeated short-term stop-start activities, not defined by timeframed measurable objectives.
NOV 2016
The FT reports a leaked memo stating an extra 30,000 civil servants are needed for 500 separate related projects

Work Smarter... Not Harder
ALLEN F. MORGENSTERN
Industrial Engineer, 1930s

SPECIFIC

Being specific is

- Carefully selecting words to provide a clear and unambiguous description or statement that everyone can understand
- Using WHO-WHAT-WHEN-WHERE-HOW-WHY to describe what you are doing

Being specific is NOT

- Always providing pages and pages of detail
- Over analysing
- Preventing changes

Many projects begin without a clearly described destination. Without the specifics, people start out with different views of where they are going and how they will get there.

Being specific means everyone will arrive at the same place at the same time!

WHAT BREXIT DID

EU REFERENDUM
Disagreement about "ignoring the democratic will of the people" as no upfront specific rules agreed
- the percentage of the vote needed to make the change
- timeframe for getting a deal voted through the UK Parliament before another referendum was needed

From *Occam's Razor Principle*
Entities should not be multiplied without necessity — The simplest solution is most likely the right one.
WILLIAM of OCKHAM
14th century friar, philosopher

SPECIFIC

Let's Begin at the Destination

Where are you going?

☐ Every project has a purpose — to make change happen.

☐ Everyone involved needs a clear commonsense description of where they will be as a result of the change

  ▪ NOT the process ...
    THE destination

  ▪ NOT Digital Transformation ...
    The DESCRIPTION of how things will be
    e.g. low cost, inclusive, innovative, agile, collaborative

☐ Include stopping off points to build a clearly defined roadmap that everyone can follow. To show ...

THE PROJECT IS HAPPENING,

HOW IT WILL BE HAPPENING

and THE DESTINATION ITSELF

Why are you going?

☐ What adds real value to your organisation or customers?

☐ What opportunities are to be found?

☐ Which problems will be solved?

☐ Which parts of the organisation will benefit?

☐ Which markets will benefit?

☐ Which products will be successful?

Why be specific?

☐ Removes ambiguity and misunderstandings

☐ Reduces dissatisfaction later if people did not understand what was planned

☐ Promotes confidence that there is a clear, well thought through plan

☐ Helps to understand where the consensus is, and where conflict may lie ahead

☐ Helps attracts people to the project team who will really support the outcome

> By prevailing over all obstacles and distractions, one may unfailingly arrive at his chosen goal or destination.
> CHRISTOPHER COLUMBUS 1451 - 1506
> Explorer

WHAT BREXIT DID

TO LEAVE OR NOT TO LEAVE
Voting paper for referendum had binary choice describing a process not the destination – to leave or to remain

Single word processes, letting people believe the journey was to their own, personal destination

Hard
BREXIT

Soft BREXIT

A Deal
Theresa
May Deal

NO DEAL

Referendum on the United Kingdom's membership of the European Union	
Vote only once by putting a cross ☒ in the box next to your choice	
Should the United Kingdom remain a member of the European Union or leave the European Union?	
Remain a member of the European Union	
Leave the European Union	

SPECIFIC
State your Destination

What can people expect?

☐ Start by being specific about what is IN and what is OUT

☐ Stand back and ask what is not included?
  - Is it needed?
  - What benefit would it add?

☐ Look at what is worth keeping e.g. collaborative culture, competitiveness, informality

☐ What will be achieved?

☐ What will be different?

OPPT FOR THE FUTURE

- How will the organisation change?
- How will people change?
- What type of technology will you be using?
- How will you need to do things differently?

Do they all work together?

DESTINATION	REMAIN	BREXIT
Key principle(s)	STATUS QUO	TAKE BACK CONTROL
Organisation	Shared legislative power with EU Parliament with European Court of Justice as Supreme Court for matters of EU law	Houses of Parliament are the makers of all legislation. Free from European Court of Justice
People	Freedom of movement for EU citizens as no internal borders, although UK elected to remain outside of Schengun agreement, so passports and border checks required	Will no longer be controlled by EU for who comes into the UK, also who can be removed, in specific circumstances. Will be much easier to recruit non-EU workers post Brexit
Process	Integrated core processes with the EU e.g. security, border controls, trade, fiscal rules	UK controlled security processes for sharing data and joint initiatives, free to develop with non-EU states
Technology	Continued use of shared EU IT systems, and joint access to new systems.	New technology solutions for shared IT systems maintained by the EU e.g. border control, nuclear assets management

WHAT BREXIT DID

FOR v AGAINST
- Public did not vote FOR a destination; the majority voted AGAINST the EU
2019 GENERAL ELECTION
- 3 words win again without being specific
TAKE BACK CONTROL becomes GET BREXIT DONE
- Morning after election analysis focuses on the specifics

NO DETAILS FOR LEAVE
- Includes A Customs Union?
- Includes THE Customs Union?
- Includes Court of Justice?

ERG and BREXIT are pro leaving groups but reject Theresa May and Boris Johnson deals as "not BREXIT"

CIVIL SERVANTS
Identified over 700 areas to be addressed to reshape the UK after leaving the EU.

- .

MEASURABLE

You have now been specific about your destination. The next step is to identify ways of monitoring your progress. Success and failure are in the eye of the beholder. The right measures provide a common ground to see progress towards the expected result and also how well the project itself is performing.

How will you know if the actual result is what was expected?

- Is it providing the expected value to customers?
- Is it providing the expected value to your organisation?
  e.g. reduced costs, increased sales, higher profitability
- What makes the project complete?
- Does the investment still match the value to be gained?

How will you know how the project itself is progressing?

- On time?   On budget?   Agreed quality?

Don't drown in the detail — know when to stop.

Measures must

- be accurate
- be of more value to you than the effort to get the information

MEASURABLE
Being Critical

What is critical to your success?

Get people involved in setting the measures for project performance and the outcome. This will get buy in and set realistic goals from the start.

Ask

- ❏ What do you need to do well?
- ❏ What do you need to avoid doing badly?
- ❏ How do others measure their success?
- ❏ What do you need to do to make you different from your competitors?
- ❏ What has already been identified in your business strategy?
- ❏ Are you delighting your customers?

How are you performing?

Once you know WHAT you need to do well, you can measure HOW well you are doing them.

- ❏ Use numbers — Quantitive measures
  Exact and can be counted

  - ≡ Time
    early/on track/late
  - ≡ Cost
    under/on target/over
  - ≡ Quality
    % errors/complaints/repeat sales

- ❏ Use words — Qualitative measures
  Not exact but can be described

  - ≡ TripAdvisor comments
  - ≡ New skills and experience

Using a combination of these measures will allow your project to have more emotional experience-based goals but be firmly based in evidence.

Critical Success Factors

Measures identifying what you need to be successful are called Critical Success Factors.
CSFs were developed by D. Ronald Daniel of McKinsey & Company in 1961 and refined into critical success factors by John F. Rockart between 1979 and 1981.
In 1995, James A. Johnson and Michael Friesen applied it to many sector settings, including healthcare.

> The key to success is hard work. You want to feel as comfortable as you can going into the game, and you do that by preparing well.
> OWEN FARRELL Born 1991
> Rugby player

WHAT BREXIT DID

WHAT IS MEASURABLE SUCCESS FOR BREXIT?
- Fiscal and investment?
- Target timeframe achieved?
- Free trade deals with rest of the world?
- Continued trading with EU?
SEPT 2018 EU's Donald Tusk Instagram with message "Maybe having their cake and eating it … with cherries"

BREXIT MANTRAS
Unmeasurable mantras designed to stir people emotionally
"Take back control"
"No downside to Brexit"
"Delivering Brexit for Britain"

"Crashing out with no deal"
"Falling off a cliff-edge with no deal"

MEASURABLE
Keeping your Balanced Scorecard

A Balanced Scorecard is a great way to measure how well the project is working, and how well the new changes work together.

Balanced measures monitor across your organisation to make sure that positive changes in one area do not create a negative impact somewhere else.

e.g. you may increase sales, but delivery errors may also increase if logistics are not also improved,

or you may get a great discount from a supplier but get supplied with poor quality product/service that creates issues

Financial
e.g. profit from sales, return from assets, running costs, supplier terms

Customer
e.g. level of customer satisfaction, reputation in marketplace, customer complaints,
% of calls to be answered within 3 minutes

Process
new/updated processes
e.g., reducing costs, lower errors

Growth/Learning/Innovation
e.g. development of new products/services, creative activity, new skills and capabilities

☐ EFFICIENCY measures look at how SPEEDILY tasks are completed.

☐ EFFECTIVENESS measures look at how WELL tasks are completed.

BALANCED SCORECARD
Robert S Kaplan and David P Norton 1996
The Balanced Scorecard is a widely used way of presenting measure.

The scorecard includes 4 different measure types to give an overall balance.

The scorecard can then be used to build dashboards to monitor performance and how changes effect other aspects of your organisation.

FINANCIAL	PROCESS
Value of the pound	New UK processes ready
Employment figures	New trade agreements
International investment	Taking back control
New global trade terms	

BREXIT BALANCED SCORECARD

CUSTOMERS	GROWTH
Polling – voter satisfaction	New technologies to replace EU systems
Protesters	New trade relationships
Faith in UK brand	

WHAT BREXIT DID

BREXIT has become a separate strand of political debate; not integrated with other goals.
e.g. NHS is key 2019 General Election issue.
Yet visa and NHS charge arrangements for EU citizens working in NHS still at proposal stage in Nov 2019 instead of securing vital resources.

BREXIT BRAVE NEW WORLD OCT 2018
Theresa May announced £120million for a Brexit Festival of Britain to showcase post Brexit Britain. Arts institutions voiced concern that post Brexit Britain would alienate many international tourists and researchers.

NO AGREED BASELINE MEASURES
Each side provides their own data on the issues they feel strongly on. No overall balanced set of measures – so some data more reliable and evidence based than others.
JULY 2016
ROD LIDDLE, Journalist
"Both sides lied! Get over it"

ACHIEVABLE

Ideas can quickly build so much momentum they become inevitable . . . the hottest technological buzz, the latest CEO enterprise. Not just the idea . . . the work itself sounds so appealing that everyone is talking about it happening. This momentum can prevent objectivity and honesty. There is a tendency to find evidence that confirms existing beliefs and assumptions, discounting or ignoring evidence that conflicts.

Sounds really obvious . . . . But think about whether the project is actually possible.

- Do you have the capacity?

  Do you really have the time, money, space, people and equipment to make it happen?

  What else is planned that will also be using the same resources?

- Do you have the capability?

  Are we telling ourselves this will be too easy?

  Do you have the right skills?

  Do you have the experience? Technically, Operationally, Commercially?

- Are you being too hesitant?

Build both aspiration and realism into your plans.

WHAT BREXIT DID

LIAM FOX, July 2017
International Trade
Secretary
"The free trade
agreement that we will
have to do with the
European Union should
be one of the easiest in
human history."

ACHIEVABLE
The Emperor's New Clothes

Look objectively at the idea before significant investment in time and energy ... before the idea has taken hold and has become inevitable.

Get a Range of Views

❑ Those directly impacted

❑ Others who are impartial and uninvolved

❑ Some with alternative views and not in favour

❑ Get the right level of detail to match the investment, potential complexity and level of risk.
e.g. informal assessment, formal Feasibility Study

Find the Problems

❑ Don't ignore issues as they will be carried forward into the project itself

❑ Research how this may been done before by someone else

EMPEROR'S NEW CLOTHES by Hans Christian Anderson
The children's story of the emperor and his followers believing his tailor had made a fabulously stylish outfit that didn't exist. The emperor and his followers were told that only the truly discerning could see the clothes.

The story is an example of Cognitive Bias, or the Bandwagon effect. People do or think things because other people do or think them.

Let our advance worries become our advance planning and thinking.
WINSTON CHURCHILL 1874 — 1965
Prime Minister and author

WHAT BREXIT DID

BINARY CHOICES
- Entrenched views from start
Leave ⟺ Remain
- Very little evidence acknowledging good on the other side, including emotive TV debates and social media exchanges
- No cross party talks after referendum to help find a workable way forward

IRISH BORDER
- Not the focus of EU Referendum debates
- Complexity ignored then has become the showstopper at the end of the negotiations

BREXIT BUS
£350million a week not called out effectively enough as not achievable before the referendum

ACHIEVABLE
Pace Yourself

Change can be exciting

Paced change shows an organisation is

- having well thought through ideas
- providing opportunities to acquire valuable new skills and experience
- investing in the future

Change can be exhausting

Set an energetic but achievable pace for all project deadlines. Too much change, implemented too quickly can

- take so much effort that exhaustion overtakes excitement
- result in failure to meet expectations
- build resentment when long standing urgent "bread and butter" Business As Usual issues are not addressed
- build a view that the organisation is badly managed

What and who would help make it happen?

- ❑ What are the opportunities to take advantage of?

What are the barriers?

- ❑ What could you remove or make less of a problem?

PORTFOLIO AND PROGRAMME MANAGEMENT

Organising projects into portfolios and programmes gives an overall view of change across an organisation.

Ensuring
- the best sequence
- the pace is managed
- there is compatibility between projects

WHAT BREXIT DID

BREXIT FATIGUE
Public increasingly losing trust with political parties to get BREXIT resolved.

PACE TOO SLOW
Public fatigue created from the extended timeline without any sign of benefit.
Quicker pace
- run up to each new deadline
- seen by some to be undermined by, the Speaker, courts, lack of direction and disagreement within both parties

NO MAJORITY
Lack of parliamentary majority and consensus slowed pace
Extreme blame game played by press and politicians instead of focussing on solutions.

RELEVANT

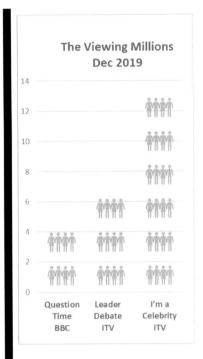

Every project has a purpose ... why it is relevant to you right now.

What makes a project relevant?

- Is it solving the right problem?   Is it solving it in the right way?
- Is there really an opportunity to make the most of?
- Should we be doing this right now? Why is it important right now?
- Once delivered, will the organisation be closer to its overall goals?
- How much value and help will the project give employees?

No organisation or project runs in isolation.   Your project may answer those questions and be very relevant to you internally, but it may not fit with what is happening outside.

- How much value and help will the project give customers?
- How much value and reassurance will the project give investors and shareholders?

Ask yourself

- Would you be better spending time and money doing something else?
- Would it be better waiting for more evidence that is the right thing to do?

The right thing at the right time for the right people

WHAT BREXIT DID

GB PUBLIC
Every political party in every election since 2004 promised a referendum in their manifestos.   Early 2016, The Telegraph records interest in Premier League football and Strictly Come Dancing far higher than interest in an EU referendum.

It must be considered that there is nothing more difficult to carry out nor more doubtful of success nor more dangerous to handle than to initiate a new order of things.
MACHIAVELLI 1469 – 1527
Author and strategist

RELEVANT

Inside and Outside

Inside

Play to your internal strengths and underplay your weaknesses

☐ What are your strengths to be exploited?

- ☑ Loyal established customer base
- ☑ Great location

☐ What are your internal weaknesses that will reduce the chance of success

- ☑ Old technology
- ☑ Unskilled staff
- ☑ Poor management information

Outside

Maximise external opportunities and avoid threats that could cause harm

☐ What are your opportunities?

- ☑ Access to funding/investment
- ☑ New technology
- ☑ Social changes
- ☑ New and emerging markets

☐ What are your threats to be managed or removed?

- ☑ Technology to help competitors
- ☑ Change to UK and global economy
- ☑ New regulations and legislation

SWOT ANALYSIS
Inside and Outside views

A SWOT analysis helps see how relevant your project is by looking at the fit both internally and externally.

Internally you can see if the project builds on your strengths but avoids exposing your current weaknesses.

Externally you can review how the project exploits opportunities and avoids threats.

Keep checking it's still relevant

		INTERNAL FACTORS
Strengths	Weaknesses	
Opportunities	Threats	EXTERNAL FACTORS

WHAT BREXIT DID

STRENGTHS
- Historic role of UK in global economy and politics
- Brand UK
WEAKNESS
- Fractured political parties
- No significant majority of opinion in country
- Both sides aggrieved and increasingly hostile

OPPORTUNITIES
- Was it the right time to take advantage of the new global markets?
THREATS
- Was it the right time to go it alone?
- Financial, shortages of goods, inflation.

LABOUR LEAVERS
- Challenge making EU relevant to some traditional Labour voters
OTHER LEAVERS
- Felt leaving would have a limited negative impact on them
- Some now feel they didn't have all the facts
- Some imply Leave voters not bright enough to understand

RELEVANT

Tell your Story

Once you have an achievable destination for your project, it needs to be sold to your audience. Successful selling needs a compelling story – a pitch. The pitch needs to tell people what to expect clearly and unambiguously.

An elevator pitch combines the specifics of your project that you have ready when you need to describe what you are doing and why.

This shows you understand the problem or the opportunity and that the project will provide real value.

- ❑ Even when no real detail exists, share what you do know.
- ❑ Don't oversell – that will only create disappointment and lose your audience.
- ❑ No jargon ... unless all your audience love jargon ... then use it! It MUST be the right pitch for the right people at the right time.
- ❑ Test it to see how people understand it, then fine tune it
- ❑ From this you can then find a quick tag line to be used in communications.

ELEVATOR PITCH
The best ideas can be explained in a few sentences.

Think about the time it takes you to travel a few floors in an elevator. How would you use the time to describe your project?

Get your pitch ready!

Test and fine tune

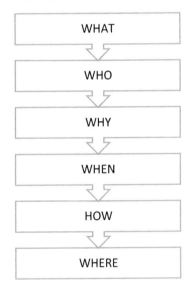

| WHAT |
| WHO |
| WHY |
| WHEN |
| HOW |
| WHERE |

WHAT BREXIT DID

PRE- REFERENDUM
Some of public were already getting Brexit fatigue by the referendum. So relevance to them lost and more focussed on reaction to quick soundbites. e.g. The input from Barack Obama often cited as reason undecided voted leave – a very human reaction to a perceived threat of bullying.

INSULAR DEBATE
Referendum campaigns and much of the debates were far beyond public understanding and interest.
e.g. about being in ... THE custom union or A custom union
Both sides used exaggerated soundbites

TOO RELEVANT
£350million for NHS displayed on BREXIT bus proved very relevant if not accurate.

TIMEFRAMED

Without a timeframe a project is not a project.

There is a timeframe for

- The project itself
- Each phase in the project
- The benefits to be received by your organisation and your customers

Build an easy to follow roadmap showing the stopping off points through your project's journey.

This gives you the targets to hit, and clear lines of failure.   Without timeframed objectives, the project lacks a sense of urgency.

WHAT BREXIT DID

TIMEFRAME
Article 50 was triggered on 29 March 2017 leading to a fixed 2 year timeframe
Followed by a series of missed BREXIT dates and extensions
- March 2019
- May 2019
- October 2019
- Jan 2020

Tomorrow belongs to those
who hear it coming
DAVIS BOWIE   1947 – 2016
Promoting the album HEROES
Artist and performer

PLAN SMARTLY
Being Objective

S	M	A	R	T
Specific	**Measurable**	**Achievable**	**Relevant**	**Time framed**

	REMAIN Elevator script	LEAVE Elevator script
WHAT What will it do?	Public British business	Public British business
WHO Who is the project is for?	Uncertainty 31 March 2019 31 October 2019 31 January 2020	Uncertainty 31 March 2019 31 October 2019 31 January 2020
WHY Why is it needed?	Benefit negotiated from large trade bloc Enable a supply of workforce Protect cultural EU identity	Economically free to do deals Sovereignty, control
WHEN When is it happening?	Strong trading union	Public fed up with perceived EU interference Unilateral federalisation
HOW How is it happening?	Do we stop it, revisit it	No deal or negotiated settlement
WHERE Where will be impacted?	United Kingdom	United Kingdom - Possibly different rules in Northern Ireland - With or without Scotland

A - Audience

Projects have an audience — the stakeholders.   These are the people and organisations with an interest in your project. They directly affect, or are affected by, your project.

Understanding each audience group will help you know how to keep them informed, interested and onside.

Looking after stakeholders well takes time, effort and thought.   Each group has different levels of influence, and will themselves have different levels of interest in your project.

- What's in it for them?

- What are their expectations?

- What will they really value to get them onside and in support of the project?

- What are their likely concerns that you can proactively prevent from becoming barriers?

Effective communication will help everyone understand what is planned and reduce potentially distracting surprises during the project.

Focus attention on those that are of most impact while making everyone feel included.   Find those that will support you and those that will resist.

AUDIENCE
Great Expectations

Who is your Audience?

☐ Who are they? How many in each group?

☐ Are there key individuals within each group?

☐ Will they benefit from the project?

☐ Will they suffer from the impact of the project?

☐ What are their key messages?

☐ How do you want to make them feel?

☐ What do you need them to do ?

☐ Who is best to build a relationship with them?

☐ What is the best way to communicate with them?

How can they Contribute?

☐ How influential are they?

☐ How interested are they?

☐ How can they help/support the project?

☐ How might they disrupt the project?

☐ How can you work proactively with the resisters and disruptors to help the project?

How will you Communicate?

☐ Tailor communications for each audience group

  ▪ How often?

  ▪ When is the best time?
    e.g. early morning, end of day, Mondays, Fridays

  ▪ What is not enough information for them? What is too much?

  ▪ What is the best way?
    e.g. emails, text, face to face, team meetings, blogs, podcasts, info packs

  ▪ What has worked well with them in the past? Ask them

☐ Plan in key checkpoints through the project when communication will be needed

☐ Schedule the communication activities needed for each group into a plan

☐ Build in ways to measure your communications — telling is not the same as listening and understanding
e.g. page visits on your intranet, opening your emails, training/workshop attendance

IT'S NOT ALL ABOUT THE PLANNING ...

In addition to a formal Communication Plan, informal unplanned spontaneous communication also has impact by making people feel noticed and involved.
e.g. impromptu walk round on a Friday afternoon, conversations in the lift or in the kitchen

But be yourself ...

I can think of nothing that an audience won't understand. The only problem is to interest them; once they are interested, they understand anything in the world.
ORSON WELLES   1915 – 1985
Film maker and actor

Powerful supporters or inflexible disruptors?

WHAT BREXIT DID

OPTICS
- House of Commons confrontational debates without end in sight hitting a low in September 2019
- News Headlines
e.g. booking of ferry companies without ships as No Deal contingency

BUSINESS
6 Mar 2019 Road Haulage Association,
17 working days left until the UK may leave the EU the Road Haulage Association is deeply concerned at the complete and utter lack of clarity.
Chris Grayling "Shut Up or Don't Engage"

NIGEL FARAGE
A loyal audience from being the master of photo opportunities
- in pubs
- BREXIT MEPs turn backs to EU anthem after EU elections
- Post referendum accuses EU of 'stealth and deception'
No one in the REMAIN team has the same audience appeal

AUDIENCE
The Outside World

External Audience

Projects may have significant stakeholders outside the organisation. Some will be an integral part of the project; some will be observers with an opinion.

- Customers
- Shareholders and Investors
- Experts
- Government departments
- Suppliers
- Trade unions
- Wider community

Your Audience has an Audience

Your audience will also have their own audience.

- ❏ Are there reasons that might influence how they work with you?
    - Are they new to their role?
    - Are they dealing with issues in their own workplace?
- ❏ Can you support their needs outside your project?
    - Can you gain their support by recognizing their position with their own audience?
    - Are there areas of mutual benefit?

THE OPTICS

The media have often asked about the OPTICS.
How will this look to ...
- voters?
- stock markets?
- the EU?

You will also have your own optics. Social responsibility is a key consideration. The way your project plays out in front of the general public will have impact. Think about how your actions and behaviours will look to a general audience.

WHAT BREXIT DID

IRELAND & NORTHERN IRELAND
- Ireland given full visible support by EU leaders as represents smaller EU nations that need to keep onside
- UK's Northern Ireland secretary Karen Bradley in post for 19 months without understanding Northern Ireland voters

EU PLAYED THEIR AUDIENCE
- David Davies photographed without folders at early negotiation meeting
- Oct 2019 Luxembourg Premiere gives press conference with an empty lectern instead of Boris Johnson
- Theresa May no match for the soundbites from the main EU communicators

EU HAS THEIR OWN AGENDA
- Macron and Merkel with support for the EU project
- Needed to make BREXIT seem negative to discourage other countries leaving e.g. FREXIT discussed by some in France, downplayed within EU and externally

AUDIENCE

Invite Your Audience

Some stakeholders will be really excited about the project; others will have little interest. Some stakeholders will have direct influence; others will have few ways of influencing the project. The STAKEHOLDER GRID will help identify where and how to focus your attention — without ignoring anybody. Focus attention on those that are of most impact while making everyone feel included. Find those that will support you and those that will resist the changes.

MANAGE ACTIVELY
High power/High interest

- Key to the outcome
- Keep informed of each step and listen to their views closely
- Where they are positive, get them to actively support and help to overcome the resisters
- Where they are negative, try to overcome objections and offset influence without blocking them out

KEEP SATISFIED
High power/Low interest

- Senior stakeholders with a wide range of interests
- Kept satisfied with progress, especially in their specific areas of interest

KEEP INFORMED
Low Power/High interest

- Usually end users
- Keep informed to generate positivity about the project across the organisation

MONITOR
Low power/Low interest

- Peripheral to outcome

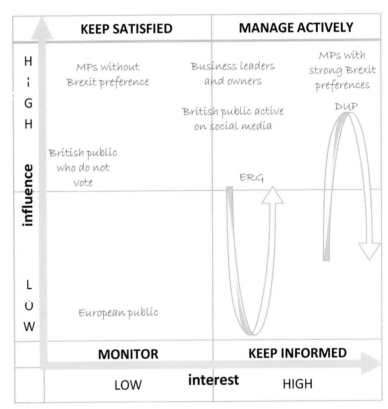

24

B   Balance

In an ideal world, projects happen fast, are cheap and produce good quality results.   In the real world there is a balance.

Successful projects balance time, costs and quality.

- Fast & Cheap NOT the Best Quality
- Cheap & Good Quality but MORE Time
- On Time and Good Quality but NOT cheap

Start by agreeing the right quality.   If your project does not meet at least minimum requirements it will not be of sufficient value to be worthwhile.

Equally the quality should not be any higher than is required when this will require higher costs and take more time.

So quality is constrained by time and cost.

Talking through this balance right from the start is central to the project.

It helps develops a mindset that you can rarely have everything — get prioritisation and compromise built in.

WHAT BREXIT DID

NO BALANCE
- No outline of the quality of deal needed to make the costs worthwhile.
- No recalculation of the benefits needed as each extension agreed.
HOW MUCH HAS THE INDECISION COST?

BALANCE

Time ⚖ Cost ⚖ Quality

Set the balance

☐ Agree the balance at the start

- Is there a fixed time the project MUST be completed by?
- At some point can the project be delivered too late?
- What are the extra costs of NOT completing on time?
- Is extra funding available if needed?
- Is there a point where the costs will increase to a point where the project needs to be stopped?
- Is there some room for compromising on the quality?
- What is the minimum level of acceptable quality? Why is that not already the scope?

Keep your balance

☐ Understanding the balance between time, quality and cost makes decision making more focussed

☐ Then assess how to re-balance when changes are agreed

☐ Any changes will need to be approved and also communicated to the wider audience

- Explain what the change is
- Explain why the change has been made
- Explain full impact i.e. budget cut means less resource and will take longer

Burning Platform
Some projects have a time constraint which will be fixed.
This can be labelled a burning platform as you have a set time to deliver the project before the platform is no longer there, and you will need a life raft.

> The dogged determination and patience of one person to do what is Right and Necessary may not always win the day or even be noticed, but it will tip the balance just a little in the direction of good.
> TERRY PRATCHETT 1948-2015
> Author

A deadline is a deadline

WHAT BREXIT DID

TIME
BREXIT was a BURNING PLATFORM, but actions leading to delays without costing impact of delays
- 2 Tory Leadership elections delaying negotiations
- 3 extensions agreed

HOW MUCH IS TIME COSTING?

QUALITY
- Compromises made on deals to try to get through House of Commons rather than looking at the benefits deal options would give
- NO DEAL recognised as falling short but accepted by some
- Reduced quality of outcome (at least in short term)

COST
- No published target cost to ensure benefits worthwhile.
- Broad brush reference to savings
- Delays mean continuing to pay EU contributions
- Visibility on true cost or accurate wealth creation virtually impossible and when produced easily rubbished !

BALANCE
Quality at any Cost?

The real cost

It can be uncomfortable and often difficult to keep track of all project costs. The full costs are needed to ensure the project is really providing value, and not being kept alive by the project team.

❏ Cost internal resources
- gives a real sense of how much the project is costing
- helps run more focussed meetings and calls — every one has a cost!

❏ Look for hidden costs
e.g. costs to end supplier contracts early

❏ Use external resources thoughtfully, encourage knowledge transfer to develop new capabilities

❏ Include costs needed for any contingencies

❏ Thoroughly identify costs after the project is completed
- Maintenance costs
- Impact of the project
  e.g. redundancy or recruitment costs

What are the options?

❏ Need to finish earlier?
- Hire more people
- Use external resources
- Buy more/better equipment
- Reduce quality
- Reduce scope

❏ Need to reduce costs?
- Reduce quality
- Reduce team size
- Re-negotiate contracts

Public information campaign

EuroTunnel out of court settlement

DUP £1 billion funding

WHAT BREXIT DID

Tangible costs

Two elections

EU referendum

C Customers

Successful organisations actively work to place the customer at the centre of their thinking and planning.

Placing the customer at the centre is an OUTSIDE-IN view.   By listening to the Voice of the Customer, products and services are more likely to be what they need, what they want and what they value.

• Gain important insights

• How do you make customers advocates, not detractors?

• What delights your customers?

• What irritates your customers?

• How do customers make their decisions?

OUTSIDE

In

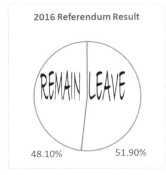

2016 Referendum Result

48.10%   51.90%

WHAT BREXIT DID

Public split into 2 distinct market segments. Each have their own view of what would add value to them.
LEAVE - EU does not add value to me
REMAIN - EU does add value to me
DIFFICULT TO FIND A SOLUTION TO MAKE BOTH HAPPY.

Listening to the Voice of the Voter shows what they value. This is different from pre-thinking how to win votes with a manifesto focussed on ideas from the party.
Listening to the Voice of the Customer builds products they value, not what looks best from inside the organisation.

CUSTOMER
Voice of the Customer

Work OUTSIDE In

☐ Think and do as the customer experiences your products and services

☐ Customers need to be part of your DNA ... ALL THE TIME

Learn about your customer

Then you can look from the OUTSIDE IN

☐ Who are your customers?

☐ How do you supply the customer what they need, what they want and what they really value?

☐ What makes your competitors success or fail?

☐ Focus on listening to the Voice of the Customer

  - Focus groups

  - Quick surveys at the point of where the customer is experiencing the product/service

  - Be a Customer yourself

  - Understand complaints

☐ Build in flexibility when market needs change

Delight your customers

Many are able to satisfy customer needs, but staying competitive means providing products and services that really impress the customer so much they come back again and again .

They also start recommending you.

Be Different

☐ As you find products and services that differentiate from competitors.

☐ As your competitors copy these differentiators you need to find the next differentiators.

☐ Let your customers help you find the next differentiators.

KANO MODEL
Noriaki Kano, Tokyo University, 1984

Focus on emotions and needs rather than just "more features = better"

Dissatisfiers - Basic Needs
- Expected features of a product or service. Without these features, the customer will be dissatisfied. e.g. hotel cleanliness

Satisfiers - Performance Needs
- Standard features that increase or decrease satisfaction. These include cost/price, ease of use, speed. e.g. how you book

Delighters - Excitement Needs
- Unexpected features that really impress customers and earn you extra recognition. e.g. chocolate on your hotel room pillow

---

> I want to top expectations. I want to blow you away.
> QUENTIN TARANTINO   Born 1963
> Film maker

WHAT BREXIT DID

VOTERS ARE CUSTOMERS
Voice of Customer not being heard
Leave voters DELIGHTED with what offered
- Remainers left frustrated on future choice taken away from them by others
- Rest of voters left deciding who makes them the least dissatisfied

VOTERS ARE CONSUMERS
- Some will still always shop or vote with the same brand
- But 2019 Election shows more voters are shopping around for "products" they value
- Parties are now seen as a brand that may or may not have a proposition for them
- Parties using marketing tools and techniques mirroring retailers

EU REFERENDUM RESULTS
Public had moved on and surprised those whose job it is to know.
Shock for
- Conservatives
- Labour
- Journalists & broadcasters
- Pollsters underestimating the impact of shy Brexiteers

CUSTOMER
Being Personal

Personas are used to represent different voices across your customers to help really empathise with what they need.

MILLENNIAL MILLY
Age: 25
Status: Single

> I will be renting for years

What's important to me:
- Social responsibility
- Climate
- Travelling
- Social Media

RETIRED REG
Age: 67
Status: Married

> Glad I have my pension

What's important to me:
- My car
- My clubs and hobbies
- My garden

NPS
Net Promoter Score measurement for customer satisfaction and loyalty

We all want to deliver excellent customer service but how do we know we are?
What does excellent customer service look and feel like for the customer?
The NPS is based on asking customers the simple question:
Would you recommend this product/service to friends and family?

> The customer may NOT always be right, however they are NEVER wrong
> ANON

WHAT BREXIT DID

PERSONAS
- Workington Man identified as key voter profile in 2019 General Election i.e. older, white, Northern man from former mining town.
- Which? BREXIT Consumer Insight segments
    Engaged and Concerned
    Hopeful Optimist
    Hopeful Pessimist
    Distant & Disengaged

Public is now fragmented market with more personas to keep happy.
- Tory/Labour Leavers
- Tory/Labour Remainers
Traditional marketing researchers role of identifying segmentations and focussing campaigns being superseded by Artificial Intelligence via social media

AGE
- Calls for voting age to be reduced to 16 for the referendum as sets the future.
- Predictions on what 2nd Referendum would be as some older voters had died and additional younger voters have turned 18

D Decisions

Successful projects need good decision making from the sponsor, the project team and the organisation itself to maintain a clearly defined direction.

Decision makers need evidence that is acknowledged as objective and valid.

People also need time to look at the evidence and make a considered decision without feeling time or internal politics is making the decision for them.

But you do need some momentum for making decisions — too much analysis can lead to paralysis and deadlock.

- Change is a constant of projects but needs to be managed
- Decisions will need to be made to keep the best balance of time:quality:cost

Pressurised decisions are more likely to become unworkable or be reversed.

WHAT BREXIT DID

VISIBLE INDECISION
- Repeated extensions
- Repeated voting for same deal without deciding what might be changed to succeed
- The key decision to leave by electorate perceived by BREXITEERS to be undermined by, Speaker and legal bodies acting outside their remit

Never thought democracy meant honouring a result I didn't expect — its thoroughly unparliamentary
OVERHEARD   June 2016
UNIDENTIFIED MP
Annie's Bar, House of Commons

DECISIONS
Making your mind up

Plan to decide

Look ahead for when key decisions are likely to be needed and make time for them in the plan.

- ❑ Get the right information to the right people to make the decision
  e.g. sales volumes for a full year or just the last month
- ❑ Make the right environment for good decision making
  - ◽ 1:1s
  - ◽ Groups sessions
- ❑ Avoid making decisions when people are tired
- ❑ Acknowledge people may be afraid to make the wrong decision and will need support
- ❑ Factor in holidays and busy times in the business

Be ready to decide

But also prepare yourself and others to make immediate unplanned decisions quickly if needed

- ❑ Know how to setup a quick meeting or conference call
- ❑ Find out how to get hold of key decision makers urgently
  e.g. talk to PAs

How to decide

- ❑ Use a method to reflect the importance of the decision
  e.g. email, formal discussion
- ❑ Make clear the difference between review time and decision time
- ❑ Get a rhythm to decision making

Keeping it logged

- ❑ Keep a decision log to reassure stakeholders that decisions are thought through and not made arbitrarily
  - ◽ When decision agreed
  - ◽ Who approved the decision
  - ◽ Supporting notes on why the decision was made
- ❑ Clear logged decision making increases the quality of decisions and helps prevents decisions being reversed

Don't let time make the decision

WHAT BREXIT DID

KEY DECISION POINTS
6 JULY 2018
Chequers Meeting
- Ministers warned if resigned would be getting a taxi home
2 APRIL 2019
7½ hour cabinet meeting
- Locked in without phones

- With little pre briefing to help make decision

LABOUR INDECISION
Trying to accommodate all views in party has come across as indecision
- Voters in traditional Labour area chose Leave
- Jeremy Corbyn is a historic Leaver
- Corbynistas are Remain voters
- Resulting in failure in 2019 General Election

NATIONAL AUDIT OFFICE DEC 2019
"With a challenge of this scale it is simply not possible for departments to plan for every eventuality. But lessons can still be learned from the previous period of no-deal planning, where in some cases rushed decisions meant taxpayers' money was not spent well. We will continue to play our role, keeping a close interest in how departments perform and report to
Parliament on risks to preparedness."

DECISIONS
You Can Leave Your Hat On

The De Bono's 6 Thinking Hats technique provides a full 360 degree of your decision.

This encourages consensus appreciating different ways of thinking about a decision.

DE BONO 6 HATS
Six Thinking Hats was designed in 1985 by Edward de Bono to be used in group and individual thinking.

EMOTIONS	INFORMATION	CREATIVE	OPTIMISM	CAUTION	PLANNING
• What is your gut reaction? • How does it make you feel?	• What are the facts?	• What's new about the proposal? • How could it be developed further?	• What are the positive benefits? • What is to be gained? • Who will gain?	• What makes you feel cautious? • What is the worst case scenario?	• What is the goal? • What is the scope?

WHAT BREXIT DID

POOR DECISIONS AND STRATEGIC ERRORS
Theresa May decides to hold an election in 2017 resulting in the loss of her majority with a disastrous impact for managing the process

FEB 2017 REACTION
Unidentified Labour MP yells - "Suicide" in the House of Commons as MPs decide to back bill to trigger the BREXIT process
EU Brexit negotiator Guy Verhofstadt to MEPs
"It is a fact that they have professionally squandered Winston Churchill's legacy"

FEB 2017 REACTION
Tory MP Iain Duncan Smith is upset by Austrian Chancellor Christian Kern re divorce bill
"For the Austrian chancellor to even refer to it is quite absurd. As for saying there's going to be no free lunch for Britain, we paid so much into the EU budget over the years, we pretty much bought the damned restaurant."

E Cause and Effect

Projects are often providing a solution to a problem.   So it is vital that the solution is solving the underlying problem.   Otherwise you will be solving the symptoms not the root cause.

The project itself will be presented with issues and again looking to root cause will be needed.

Close down endless talking about the "problem" and use structured evidence gathering without having blame as the focus.   Then you will fully understand the issue and agree the best solution.

How do you see the effect?

- Results below expectation?

- Results below a required standard e.g. a SLA?

- Results are inconsistent?

CAUSE AND EFFECT
Stating the obvious and not so obvious

A Problem Statement is a brief clear description of what the problem is.

❑ What is the problem?
  - What is happening?
  - What is it affecting?
  - Who/what is affected by the problem?
❑ How important is the impact?
  - Costing money
  - Lowering quality
  - Inconsistent quality
  - Breaking compliance rules
  - Compromising safety
❑ How urgent?
  - When will it become serious?
  - Why is it a problem now?
  - Is it getting worse?
  - Is there a pattern?
    All the time?
    Triggered by something?

Breakdown barriers
Fully understanding the root cause takes time, patience and often diplomacy.

❑ Collate information to understand the problem
❑ Bring new people into the conversation

> Between good sense and good taste there lies the difference between a cause and its effect
> JEAN DE LA BRUYERE   1546 – 1696
> Philosopher

We've always done it this way – it works

We don't have resource to look at this

Its too complicated to change

KEN CLARKE
Although David Cameron saw the EU Referendum as finally solving divisions in the Tory party, it resulted in stalwarts of the party having the whip removed in September 2019.

WHAT BREXIT DID

DAVID CAMERON
- Sees the division in the Tory party is getting worse following EU FINANCE REGULATIONS in 2011 with UK veto ignored.
- Decided to address with a "once in a lifetime" referendum promised by Tony Blair in 2004-5.

2019 ELECTION RESULT
- Was BREXIT the cause of the Labour failure?
Or
- HAS BREXIT been an effect of other changes in society?

This needs to be resolved for Labour to solve the right problem and re-gain their position.

CAUSE AND EFFECT
Why? Why? Why? Why? Why?

☐ Start with a question about why the problem occurs

☐ Then ask what causes that

☐ Continue until you have discovered the root cause

☐ Then you can ask what solutions can be used for the root cause

Fix the cause not the symptoms

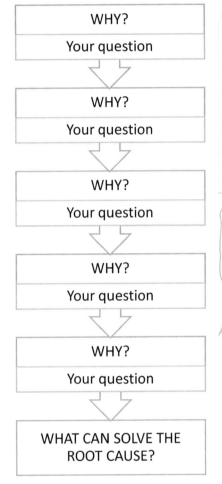

| WHY? |
| Your question |

| WHY? |
| Your question |

| WHY? |
| Your question |

| WHY? |
| Your question |

| WHY? |
| Your question |

| WHAT CAN SOLVE THE ROOT CAUSE? |

5 WHYs

Developed in the 1930s by Toyota Industries to solve production problems with multiple root causes.

The 5 WHYS tool can be used at any time during the project to identify the root cause of problem, or may include the overall project problem.

ANON
Solve the problem or leave the problem.
Do not live with the problem.

WHAT BREXIT DID

IRISH BORDER
- Lots of useful initial talk between respective border authorities North and South-but not followed through by government

BREXIT EFFECT ON EU
- Vote lent support to anti-Establishment, anti-EU bodies feeling across Europe. Brexit vote result has empowered and will empower these groups
- UK leaving may further fragment EU and possibly encourage others to leave
- Will impact EU financially

EU - OTHER EFFECTS
Vote widely considered most significant European event since fall of Berlin Wall 1989. By 2016 EU impacted by a number of damaging events.
- Global economic crisis 2008
- Failure to deal with euro flaws
- Russia upsets cold war balance
- Terrorism
- Large migration flows

F Finish

A good route map has a final destination with the stopping off points clearly marked.

The stopping off points are where you can stop and review where you are.

- What has been achieved?
- Is the running of the project working?
- Is the final destination still the same?

The FINISH at the final destination is not the BIG GO LIVE.   There is no finishing post. It is the end of a project with recognition that the changes are now the new normal and benefits have started to be seen.

This needs to be recognised and prepared for.

- How will you know when the project is finished and works needs to happen as Business as Usual?
- What needs to be done once there?

Building in the finish right from the start develops a sense of ownership and responsibility with the ultimate owners.   The project is the facilitator — not the owner.   It also ensures the project team includes a complete handover.

Nothing at the end should be a real surprise.

WHAT BREXIT DID

NO REAL GO LIVE
- No confirmed workable lead-time for any of the deadlines
- So no one knows what they are getting ready for
- Leading to loss of confidence

The greatest results in life are usually attained by common sense and perseverance.
OWEN FELTHAM   1602 - 1668

FINISH

Are we there yet?

Go-No-Go

After all the hard work you will finally arrive at the switch on.

Have a clear checklist to be sure that all is well to go ahead with the change.

- ☐ Tasks that must be completed before GO LIVE
  - ▪ testing completed to agreed standard
  - ▪ new procedures documented
  - ▪ incorporated in future Business As Usual budgets
- ☐ Give people enough time to prepare their teams
  - ▪ training
  - ▪ recruitment
- ☐ Contingency ready, tested and understood if there are issues after GO LIVE
- ☐ Feedback routes setup and known by all

Going LIVE!

There are different approaches to implementing your changes.

- ☐ Phased — gradual rollout across your organisation
- ☐ Big bang — single one off implementation across the organisation
- ☐ Pilot — try in one part of organisation and learn from experience.

Go LIVE!

- ☐ Review across the stakeholders and agree a GO
- ☐ Start to LIVE the changes

BEWARE FALSE STARTS

Getting people ready and then delaying the GO LIVE is difficult to manage.

WHAT BREXIT DID

GO LIVE
No proactive thought about how to Go Live.
- Big Bang v Phased not looked at to demonstrate support for business in UK & EU
2019 GENERAL ELECTION
- Win largely attributed to GET BREXIT DONE. But Finish still unclear until trade negotiations complete.

Commenting on the launch of Public Information Readiness Campaign in August 2019 when still without a deal, Business Secretary Andrea Leadsom said:
'The UK will be leaving the EU on 31 October. For businesses that still feel unprepared, I am determined to do everything I possibly can to ensure they are fully ready for Brexit.'

EUROTUNNEL PAYOUT
- EuroTunnel planned an effective Business Readiness Plan after referendum for GO LIVE
- sued the government for £33 million to settle lawsuit over extra ferry services
- Then P&O sue government over settlement putting it at a competitive disadvantage

FINISH
Tidy Up Before You GO-GO

Prepare for your end

- ❏ Create a Transition Plan to describe how you will close the project with tasks and knowledge to transfer from the project team and suppliers to Business as Usual teams.
    - ⬛ What needs to be handed over?
    - ⬛ Who needs to have a handover?
    - ⬛ When should the project team resources be stood down or re-deployed?
    - ⬛ What could be included to really delight the stakeholders?
    - ⬛ What are the final lessons learned?
    - ⬛ How will the end result be communicated across the organisation?
- ❏ Agreement that the deliverables are complete and as expected
- ❏ Agree a date after the Go Live e.g. access to systems and documentation
- ❏ Schedule tasks to ensure the changes are sustained after 3 months etc e.g. new Ways of Working are being fully utilised, continuous improvement demonstrated
- ❏ Reconcile all the finances

What happens next?

- ❏ Agree to complete anything incomplete as business-as-usual
- ❏ New ways of working are on the way to being established as the norm
- ❏ Benefits will continue to be realised and managed over time
- ❏ Continuous improvement can build on the project's gains

CELEBRATE GOOD TIMES

- ❏ Find the right time to celebrate success.
    - ⬛ After GO LIVE and efforts to bed in
    - ⬛ Before the resources get disbanded

UNEXPECTED FINISH

Always be prepared to stop before the expected date.
Some projects are stopped due to external factors
e.g. a merger, recession

Others just become unrecoverable, and it is clear the costs will now exceed the expected benefits.
- The costs have changed
- The benefits were over estimated

WHAT BREXIT DID

BREXIT DAY is not Go live
- It is not all over with BREXIT DAY
- Focus on BREXIT DAY but the complex negotiations are still to do
- This is just the Divorce Settlement
- Ongoing relationship still to be agreed and not fully outlined in 2019 Election debates

UNFINISHED
- Messy transition so public & business left with misgivings

Go Live is NOT the end

G Governance

You can delight the customers; you can keep stakeholders happy but you will get nowhere without the right people approving your way.

Governance is a careful balance between freedom to get on with projects and compliance to ensure fixed rules are followed.   The approach should fit the project. Innovation projects may find traditional governance models restrictive, but still need some level of control.

Good governance processes ensure:

- The right projects are selected
- The right decisions are made
- A natural cycle of approval is followed

Governance rules must be understood across all involved so that focus always stays on the outcome of the project - not on disputes about who makes decisions and how they are made.

- What decisions and approvals are controlled within the project team?
- What decisions and approvals are controlled outside the project team?

  From specialist teams   e.g. IT, Finance, Health & Safety

  From external compliance   e.g. FCA, Sarbanes–Oxley

Control who needs to be involved in decisions internally and externally.

GOVERNANCE
What are the rules?

Know your Route

Confirm any governance you must use FROM THE START.   This prevents delays and distractions at key points when approval is needed but route is unclear

- ❑ Confirm the detail of the internal Governance needed
- ❑ if already in place, fully understand what are the routes you need to manage
  - ⚞ Project spend
  - ⚞ IT spend
  - ⚞ Recruitment of resources
- ❑ If no formal governance in place, setup to match the type of project

Plan Your Route

Make it easy for approvers to work with you.

- ❑ Make contact with the key approvers to get tips on what they need when approving
  e.g. numbers, discussion
- ❑ Schedule dates for approval and review in your plan, and in approvers' diaries
- ❑ Circulate pre-read information and then give time for open discussion
- ❑ Confirm role of contractors and consultants in key decision making
- ❑ Involve those with the ongoing Business As Usual ownership

CONTRACTS

Governance also covers contracts with external suppliers.
Take time to review all the detail.
- Is there enough information to describe the product/service to be supplied?
- How can you end the contract?
- What are the Key Performance Indicators and Service Level Agreements?
- What happens if these are not being met?

WHAT BREXIT DID

TACTICAL VOTING DECISION NOV 2019 THE GUARDIAN
- 3 REMAIN tactical voting websites use data driven decision making for how to vote in the 2019 BREXIT General Election.
- fail to agree on advice

GOVERNANCE TRADITIONS
- BREXIT has demonstrated how much government is still routed in the past.
- The paper for the meaningful vote was on paper NOT digital with the Yes/No as Aye/ No
- Some MPs stand through the long crucial debates as the chamber does not have enough seats for all 650 MPs

GOVERNANCE
Key Players

Internal
- ❏ Main Board
- ❏ Legal and Compliance
- ❏ Finance
- ❏ HR
- ❏ Chief Technical Officer
- ❏ Operations
- ❏ Customer Care
- ❏ Marketing
- ❏ Workforce, Trade Unions

External
- ❏ Regulators
  - ☑ FCA for Financial Services
  - ☑ GDPR for data sharing
  - ☑ Saubonne-Oxley for Accounting
- ❏ Investors
- ❏ Experts

WHAT BREXIT DID

GINA MILLER'S LEGAL CHALLENGES
NOV 2016   The High Court of Justice rule that Parliament had to legislate before the Government could invoke Article 50.
SEP 2018   The High Court uphold the decision to suspend Parliament was unlawful.

BORIS JOHNSON STRATEGY
- Each element challenged
- in-House of Commons
- then challenged in law courts
- proroguing of Parliament carried out in a ceremony at 1:15am in traditional costume
- then proroguing reversed less than a month away from 31 October deadline
- Ending with success of majority in 2019 Election

THE BERCOW FACTOR
The Speaker
Perceived as biased
- popular with Remainers,
- unpopular with Brexiteers
- stretching precedence and Parliamentary rules
- new Speaker applicants stress neutrality during appointment process

H History

Very few projects start from Year 0. They start with memories of yesterday.

Experience from previous projects and also the reputation of the people involved are a legacy of successes and failures … and all things in between.

This all provides the context, and preconceptions, of how any project will be delivered.

Your own project is also making its own history.   Learn as you go — from the good and the bad.

WHAT BREXIT DID

It's argued that levels of service have declined greatly leading to a lack of confidence in our politicians – some of the public (the customers) seek alternatives like Nigel Farage
e.g. MP expenses scandal still fresh as we had the EU referendum

Any fool can know, the point is to understand
ALBERT EINSTEIN 1879 – 1955
Scientist

HISTORY
What went on before ...

Projects

Examine other projects in your own organisation and by Googling for projects outside your organisation.

☐ Is there a proven track record of success or failure?

☐ Were projects delivered ... ?

- ☑ As expected
- ☑ On time
- ☑ On budget

☐ How were the projects delivered ...?

- ☑ was everyone involved?
- ☑ was it all controlled by a small project team?

☐ What is still being talked about ... ?

- ☑ That went well?
- ☑ That went badly?

☐ Acknowledge past experiences and look for ways to address

☐ What other projects have the project manager and team delivered before?

☐ Are external resources involved?

- ☑ What has been the track record of using external resources — contractors or consultancies?

☐ Is this yet another in a series of CEO vanity projects?

Making Your Own History

☐ Don't wait until the end of the project to learn lessons — do when memories are fresh and you can benefit immediately

- ☑ Cloud-based EXCEL list or TRELLO board
- ☑ Writeable visible space in office

☐ Have checkpoints throughout the project and ways for people to add as they think of them. e.g. meeting agenda item

> Insanity is doing the same thing over and over again and expecting different results
> ALBERT EINSTEIN   1879 — 1955
> Scientist

WHAT BREXIT DID

PROJECTS
- Windrush
- Grenfell response
- Olympics lack of legacy
- NHS systems project
- Universal Credit rollout
- MPS Expenses scandal
- HS2 behind and overspent
- Crossrail behind and overspent
- Carillion collapse

PEOPLE-THERESA MAY
JULY,2016 Ken Clarke
"bloody difficult woman"
As Home Secretary
- Indecisive & non collaborative
e.g. Police conference PR
disaster
OCT 2017
- Handed P45 at conference
by comedian Lee Nelson

PEOPLE-JEREMY CORBYN
- historic Leaver used as reference point in the debate
- supported Irish vote not to ratify Lisbon Treaty in 2007
"such a boost to people like us" who "do not want to live in a European empire of the 21st century"
- appears indecisive about honouring referendum after campaigning that he would

HISTORY
Déjà Vu

<table>
<tr><td>

1530s
REFORMATION

- After years of trying to a get a deal on the royal divorce, the UK takes back control from the European Catholic church

</td><td>

1990
NO NO NO

- Margaret Thatcher responded to the Maastricht Treaty as the European Parliament called to be the democratic body of the European Community
- Triggers a split in the Tory party

</td></tr>
</table>

1640s
THE CIVIL WAR

Split the Union of the United Kingdom

Split friends and family

Split over who had the governance in Ireland

1700s   PATRIOTS

First Euro-Sceptics that launched Rule Britannia as an anthem led by the Prince of Wales

Wanted freedom to trade

1815-1846
CORN LAWS

Lower tariffs splits the Tories Conservative PM Sir Robert Peel uses Whig support to repeal

1900s
FREE TRADE

Joseph Chamberlain resigned from the Tory Cabinet to campaign for tariffs, supported by Irish Unionist MPs

1950s, 1960s
COMMON MARKET

Harold Macmillan's request to join rejected

WHAT BREXIT DID

SOME OF BRITAIN FRUSTARTED BY EU
- Sovereign and bank debt
- Euro factor
- China factor
- Russia factor
- Fear of migration factor
- Eurozone fiscal rigidity

IRELAND
History would suggest Ireland would be a key consideration
- circumstances of Ireland's independence,
- The Troubles followed by the Good Friday Agreement
- Impact of recent global recession on Ireland
BUT NOT A MAJOR FEATURE OF REFERENDUM DEBATES

LESSONS LEARNED?
Are the learnings from project Brexit being passed on for other government projects?
e.g.HS2
    3 September 2019 Delayed by 5 years
    - £20bn overspend
Carillion collapsed with continued government support in run up, 2 hospitals shelved

I Impact

Every project has predictable impacts — positive and negative. All impact, even positive change, needs managing. Your change may successfully increase sales but this is likely to impact customer contact centre workload.

Some impacts add or remove costs; others increase or minimise risks.

Identifying, assessing and acknowledging the impacts help set the pace for change:

What capabilities are needed?

- Do they exist already or will they need to be developed?

What is the capacity?

- What else is happening? Enough resource to do this project as well?

- What will the impact be on the day-to-day business-as-usual workload?

How complex is the new project?

- Will it be easy to plan, understand and implement?

The impact needs to be continually assessed — the world changes while the project is happening.

Projects may also start a chain reaction of unexpected impacts that are not easily predicted.

WHAT BREXIT DID

OTHER WORK DELAYED
- BREXIT prioritised attention and budgets
- Absorbed energy
- BREXIT consumed Parliamentary time
- Debates delayed due to volume of BREXIT debate
- Transfer of Civil Servants into Project BREXIT

IMPACT
Setting the Pace

What's the Impact?

Upfront impact analysis helps to have a smooth running plan without re-planning to cope with lack of resources.

Talk though what is planned with those involved.

- End users
- Support services
- Suppliers
- Customers

☐ Get each group to confirm how they predict they will be impacted

☐ Test with extremes of good/bad impact

What's the right pace?

Confirm what may be needed to offset the impact and then how much change can come happen.

☐ Complexity?
  - Will it be easy to plan, understand and implement?

☐ Capability
  - Do your already have the right skills and experience or will need to be developed?
  - Will you need to recruit people with the skills and experience?

☐ Capacity?
  - What else is happening?
  - Is there enough resource to do this project aswell?
  - What will the impact be on the day-to-day business-as-usual workload?
  - Is there enough space to locate additional people?
  - What additional equipment is needed? e.g. laptops, printers, kitchen facilities

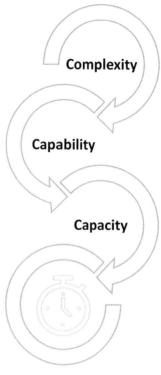

Complexity

Capability

Capacity

Set your Pace

WHAT BREXIT DID

IMPACT ASSESSMENT
- No clear impact assessment published pre referendum
- Civil Service YELLOWHAMMER report on contingency planning not seen as trusted source by all
- Public Information campaign starts in September 2019 when outcome, and therefore impact, still unknown.

NON BREXIT ISSUES
- Climate change
- NHS has record waiting lists
- Flammable cladding still on buildings in the UK 2½ years after the Grenfell fire
- Impact of AI for economy, education and society
- No time to action learnings from Monarch airlines before Thomas Cook collapse

COMPLEXITY
Not fully appreciated that disintegration is so much harder and more complicated than integration
i.e. leaving harder than joining

Joining you are GIVEN choices;
Leaving you have to MAKE the choices

IMPACT
The Butterfly Effect

Be Prepared

Planned changes may trigger other impacts that have not been predicted. Unplanned changes may unsettle the project.

Spend time looking for potential impacts of the changes you are making.

Be prepared to react to unplanned impact — good and bad!

e.g. location to new improved offices may increase staff turnover if other similar jobs are now available

What could be impacted?

Look at what could be impacted and then ask what impact those changes might make.

❑ Organisation
- New structure
- New culture e.g. less formal

❑ Process
- More complexity
- Higher/lower volumes
- Different timing
- Different sequencing
- Ways of working

❑ People
- Updated roles & responsibilities
- New job descriptions
- Recruitment

❑ Technology
- From manual to automated AI
- From paper to digital
- From desktops to new touch screen tablets

BUTTERFLY EFFECT

Describes the results of small changes on larger events. The butterfly metaphor was derived from Edward Norton Lorenz's work. His Strange Attractor chart plotted in the shape of a butterfly.

Does the Flap of a Butterfly's Wings in Brazil set off a Tornado in Texas?

WHAT BREXIT DID

THE UNEXPECTED
David Cameron sets referendum to bring closure .and unity
- yet now set us on years of division
- talk of existential Tory crisis, then spreading even to the Labour party
- gives Liberals new life and purpose with Remain option

FIXED TERM PARLIAMENT ACT
- Put in place to as part of deal between Conservative-Liberal Coalition Government
- But then prevents Boris Johnson calling an election to get majority in a new parliament

THE UNION at RISK
Northern Ireland
- focus on the Irish border gives Irish Nationalists a new voice
Scotland
- Remain majority and then 2019 Election result gives impetus for another Independence Referendum
Wales
- Scotland has re-focussed Welsh independence

J Jargon

Every project develops its own language.

Some words and phrases will be specific to the project, and others will be new words and jargon from the outside world.

Within the project team, the jargon gets adopted much faster then throughout the rest of the organisation. This builds a barrier that turns people off people and encourages the project to become disconnected.

Handled positively jargon can be introduced to add to knowledge.

Increased knowledge will enable users to more fully participate:

- providing better information
- asking the right questions

WHAT BREXIT DID

BREXIT has spawned a huge amount of its own language including the word BREXIT itself. Project speak has included BREXIT MEANS BREXIT yet still confusion in Dec 2019 about what BREXIT is in detail.

Bad terminology is the enemy of good thinking. When companies or investment professionals use terms such as 'EBITDA' and 'pro forma,' they want you to unthinkingly accept concepts that are dangerously flawed.
WARREN BUFFETT   Born 1930
Business leader and philanthropist

JARGON
Speaking Project-ese

Projects can generate and spread high volumes of jargon

❑ Business terms

❑ Technical terms

❑ Acronyms

❑ Analogies

e.g. an opportunity NOT a problem, burning platform

Break Down the Barriers

❑ Set an example of how to communicate to make sure that jargon does not create a barrier

▪ Don't hide behind jargon

▪ Don't use jargon to dress up what you are doing as this is likely to undermine your message

▪ Don't let others fee they have to learn YOUR language to communicate to you

❑ Encourage people to question what they don't understand

❑ Keep it simple but don't apologise for using new language

❑ If really necessary, set up a glossary for people to add to

❑ Check for any new jargon that may get confused with existing organisation speak

Nigel Farage speaks against the Westminster bubble

Ours is the age of substitutes: Instead of language we have jargon; instead of principles, slogans; and instead of genuine ideas, bright suggestions."

ERIC BENTLEY   Born 1916
Critic and playwright

WHAT BREXIT DID

WESTMINSTER BUBBLE
- Jargon alienates public and make them suspicious of both politicians and journalists as even the media is guilty itself of using (and inventing) jargon
- At a time of low confidence in politicians and frustration at delays, the introduction of new terminology unwelcome

NOT TALKING THE SAME LANGUAGE
- UK talk about a **deal**; EU talks about a **treaty**
- Benn Act referred to as Surrender Act by Boris Johnson
- Proroguing in Sept 2019
   is legal ?
   is illegal ?
- Remoaners not Remainers

RISE OF GENERAL JARGON
Words and phrases like
- Optics
- Feet to the Fire
- Skin in the Game
- Cherry Picking

JARGON

Word Up

- How do actions play out to the public?
- What will be on the opening of the news or go viral?

OPTICS

- Ancient test of courage or torture
- Now a test of commitment to cause

FEET TO FIRE

- Person or group involved in current actions
- Impacted by risks involved in achieving the goal

SKIN IN THE GAME

- Media name for a protocol appended to the draft Withdrawal Agreement in 2017
- To prevent a border with customs control

BACKSTOP

- Legislation by Labour MP Hilary Benn
- Boris Johnson had to reach a deal or gain Commons' approval for No Deal by Oct 19

BENN ACT

- Cabinet members must publicly support decisions made in Cabinet
- Even if they do not privately agree

CABINET COLLECTIVE RESPONSIBILITY

- Alternative name for a No-deal Brexit
- No agreements in place predicted to cause chaos at ports and across business

CRASH OUT

- Norway and Canada are given as examples of solutions for trade agreement between the EU and non-EU countries

DEALS

- The money due to the EU on UK exit
- Negative terminology – as no one considers a divorce bill in a positive light

DIVORCE BILL

- UK Government motion to approve the Withdrawal Agreement and framework for the future

MEANINGFUL VOTE

- Outline ideas from Brexit talks between Boris Johnson's team and the EU
- Indicating they were not concrete

NON PAPER

- End of a parliamentary session
- Prorogued until next session's State Opening of Parliament

PROROGUE

- To present an obstacle to ...
- "motivated by the improper purpose of stymying parliament" SUPREME COURT

STYMYING

- Practical arrangements for how UK leaves Includes a transition period & an OUTLINE of the future

WITHDRAWAL AGREEMENT

- Organisation used for the regulation of international trade
- Largest economic organisation in the world

WTO World Trade Organisation

K Keep on Track

You get one chance to start your project with the right foundation for success and the best chance of keeping on track.

- Establish effective Ways of Working for the project
- Establish robust project processes
- Agree format and list of documentation required

You will have to react to change as the project continues, but by establishing a foundation for the project you are limiting own goals from within the project itself that may knock you off track.

Through the project take time to look at how the project work is running.

- What are the measures you can use to see if you are still on track?
- What can you ask and look for to check if people are still on board?

KEEP ON TRACK
Best Foot Forward

Setup for Success

- ❑ Start with a launch meeting with the wider project team

  - ◦ Get the sponsor to come and speak about why the project is important to them

  - ◦ Get people to introduce themselves
    What they will be doing and what they have been doing
    What they are most looking forward to
    What they are NOT looking forward to

- ❑ Assign responsibilities across the team

  - ◦ Documentation

  - ◦ Communication

  - ◦ Change

  - ◦ Championing benefits

Building Success

- ❑ Make opportunities to acknowledge the importance of each person and the project overall

- ❑ Keep everyone updated on progress

Set your Ways of Working

- ❑ Promote, demonstrate and embed how you want the project to run
  e.g. homeworking, visual planning

- ❑ Decide

  - ◦ How much confidentiality is needed

  - ◦ Core working hours

  - ◦ Meeting schedule and styles
    e.g. stand-ups, digital comms

  - ◦ How to share knowledge

- ❑ Make it clear how decisions will be made

  - ◦ How to control change

  - ◦ Your governance and approvals for sign-offs and budget

- ❑ How to log Lessons Learned for improving your own and future projects

- ❑ Setup

  - ◦ Ready made templates for key documents

  - ◦ List of mandatory documents for the project type
    e.g. business case, requirements catalogue

WHAT BREXIT DID

COMMUNICATION
No formal communication plan set in place
- with public
- with media
- with parliament

SEP 2016 House of Commons
- Theresa May "We will not provide a running commentary on Brexit negotiations"

SETUP FOR FAILURE
Cabinet not established as solid project team
- Lack of cabinet responsibility
- Different briefings and interpretations from within project team ... the cabinet
- Resignations of key project members with opportunity to vent their opinions
All leading to no foundation for success

LACK OF INVOLVEMENT
Very limited lines of engagement setup for
- cross party involvement
            until too late then appeared grudgingly
- other important stakeholders
CBI, Trade Unions, Customs, NHS

KEEP ON TRACK
How is it going?

How do you know all is well?

Your progress needs to be assessed at points in time and also by looking at trends.

- Cost
  - How much money has been spent?
  - Is the budget being spent faster/slower than planned?

- Time
  - Is the project progressing faster/slower than planned?
  - How much work has been completed?

- Changes
  - How many changes requested?
  - Has the scope increased?
  - Is the contingency being used?
  - How many risks are unmanaged?

- Tasks
  - How many tasks completed?
  - Compared to planned?
  - Is the project dealing with more issues?
  - Is the project becoming more risky?

- Benefits
  - Are the benefits being delivered at the rate and quality expected?

How do people feel?

- About the pace?
  - Is there project fatigue?
  - More resource needed?
  - More Quick Wins needed to fully demonstrate progress?

- About the planned outcome?
  - Will it happen?
  - Will it happen but with compromises?

CHECKPOINT REPORTS
Keep everyone updated with progress.
- Confirm what is on track using clear measures e.g. %completed
- Alert any concerns

Tailor reports to include what will be of interest to different stakeholders, and how they would like to hear about progress.
e.g. some will value a personal weekly call, others will value a brief structured email they can read in their own time

If there is no struggle, there is no progress.
FREDERICK DOUGLASS   1818 — 1895
American social reformer

WHAT BREXIT DID

SNAKES AND LADDERS
- Difficult to track progress when plan redrawn and reset so many times
- No regular status reports to the public

SLOW THEN FAST
Lost momentum
- Tory leadership election after referendum in June 2019
- Another Tory leadership election after MEP elections in May 2019

BREXIT FATIGUE
Large sections of public have switched off and are no longer sure it will ever happen

Some have changed mind
- from REMAIN to BREXIT just to get out of stalemate
- From BREXIT to REMAIN as worried about No Deal

KEEP ON TRACK
Change Reaction

What is happening?

Projects will not go to plan. FACT.

- Some things will go better than expected; some will not go as planned

- You may also need to respond to changes from inside the project, organisation and external world.

- Triggered by changes
  - Organisation changes reduces or eliminates need
  - Budget cuts
  - Needed sooner than planned

- React to project not progressing to plan
  - Late
  - Over budget
  - Quality issues e.g. settled software not performing as expected

What's failing?

- Projects are unlikely to stick to the plan

- Expect some variance, but use measures to understand the impact
  - What are the implications? Time – Cost – Quality
  - By how much?

- Understand why the project is failing
  - Poor performance by team or supplier?
  - Wrong resources?
  - Changing needs?

What is to be done?

Effective reaction to changes is a significant factor in a project's ultimate success

- Don't wait too long

- See if can be saved Time – Cost – Quality

- Fully understand the change

- Look at options and discuss with stakeholders

- Escalation needs to be balanced
  - If escalate every issue will lose impact when REALLY important
  - But need to escalate when you need help

100 DAYS PLAN

One approach to reset a failing project is to implement a 100 Days Plan.
- Set a timeframe to suit the project
- Micro manage tasks to a daily schedule

This will create focus and a sense of urgency. It will also be really clear when tasks slip, making it easier to resolve root cause of short comings and failures.

> How did it get so late so soon ?
> DR SEUSS   1904 – 1991
> Author

We have an issue ...

↓

The implications are ...

↓

If we could ...

↓

It could be resolved by ...

WHAT BREXIT DID

UNEXPECTED ELECTION RESULTS
- Confidence in politicians starts to decline
- Loss of working majority
- Article 50 enacted before negotiating tactics agreed
- No contingency for negative outcome
- Government always on back foot

WITHDRAWAL AGREEMENT
- ATTEMPTS TO AGREE
- Theresa May tries three times to get vote through without much adjustment to tactics.
- Speaker perceived by some to be going beyond speakers powers
- Supreme Court perceived by some to be going beyond accepted deference to supremacy of Parliament

BREXIT FAILING
- Sticking points not addressed, DUP and Tory concerns over backstop
- Leaked Yellowhammer report raises prospect of medical and food shortages
- Repeated attempts to resolve via election frustrated

L Leadership

Sound and efficient sponsors and project managers can deliver successful projects; great projects need great leadership.   Team belief and performance is key for project delivery. Great leaders give energy and purpose to those taking part in the project.

Leadership is needed at many levels throughout a project.   The Sponsor has the vision; the Project Manager keeps all on track; Team Leads promote the project; and third parties help to enable the change.

Leaders set direction with an inspiring vision to create something new.

Support is needed through difficult times; pride and praise is needed for the good times.

Some projects are able to cope without an energising leader; others need a leader who will inspire and lead the way.   Leadership is often at its most powerful when authentically drawn from personal challenges and experiences. Undoubtedly it backfires if contrived and seen as not being authentic.

LEADERSHIP
Follow Your Leader

Demonstrate leadership

- ❑ Share
  - ⊠ Vision
  - ⊠ Success
  - ⊠ Problems and failure
- ❑ Be decisive
  - ⊠ Promote consensus
  - ⊠ Focus on the end game
- ❑ Keep momentum

Be authentic

- ❑ Teams value leaders showing real empathy and personality
  - ⊠ being seen on the ground directly interacting with people
    e.g. teams being re-located, customers buying new products or services
  - ⊠ GENUINELY AUTHENTIC and VALUED experiences not INVENTED, STAGE MANAGED ones
- ❑ Show personal gratitude
  e.g. eating the breakfast butties with the team not just buying them
- ❑ Be visible when difficult messages are being shared, going beyond sending an email
- ❑ Create environment where people can be listened to
  - ⊠ Interactive meetings
  - ⊠ 1:1s
  - ⊠ Approachable and spontaneous

> Leadership is the art of getting someone else to do something you want done because he wants to do it.
> DWIGHT D. EISENHOWER 1890-1969
> US President

Leaders lead the way

LEADERSHIP PHOTO OPPORTUNITY
Sept 2019 – day after election
Rescue dog Dilyn arrives at
No 10 to live with Boris Johnson,
and seen again on 2019 Election
Day`

WHAT BREXIT DID

DAVID CAMERON
Corporate leadership style
- "Call Me Dave"
- Bad tempered interviews
- Resigned the day after EU referendum result
- largely accepted would have quickly become untenable to stay
- Blamed by all including Danny Dyer

CABINET COLLECTIVE RESPONSIBILITY
- Each reshuffle failed to establish Theresa May's leadership
- Seeking consensus however party and Parliament dysfunctional

BORIS
LEADER OR LIABILITY?
- Past held against him
- Laughed at when asked about trustworthy-ness on TV debate
- Avoiding 2019 Leader debates
BUT
- Quickly established message discipline in cabinet and party
- Did get a deal as promised
- Got the Commons majority needed in 2019 Election

LEADERSHIP

> Bob [Paisley] and I never had any rows.
> We didn't have any time for that.
> We had to plan where we were going to keep all
> the cups we won.
> **BILL SHANKLY 1913-1981**
> Footballer and Football Manager

Share glory and failure

WHAT BREXIT

LEO VARADKAR
Taoiseach of Ireland

Right place   Right time
- Support from US and EU
- Recognises and maximises that country most likely to be impacted by hard Brexit
- Spectre of The Troubles returning

ANGELA MERKEL
Shows empathy on visit to Ireland in April 2019, and reiterates EU support for Ireland
"For 34 years I lived behind the Iron Curtain so I know only too well what it means once borders vanish, once walls fall"
"Germany stands with Ireland"

EU STRONG LEADERSHIP
- EU decision making centralised in Brussels and effective across 27 countries
- EU baffled by lack of continuity as different Brexit ministers keep resigning
BUT
- Responded quickly to Boris Johnson becoming PM with some flexibility with own red lines

M Make it Happen

Projects create change.   By managing the change, opportunities are maximised and issues minimised.

Even when the project is wanted and needed, thinking about how to manage the change is still really beneficial, sometimes necessary.

The organisation itself will change, and individuals will find their work experience changed.

These changes are a combination of

- Knowledge e.g. new processes, new products, new policies
- Emotions e.g. adapting to new ways of working, new location, uncertainty

Enabling change needs

- A clear vision showing how the change is relevant without over communicating
- Leadership
- Support from those with skills and experience to help
- Opportunities for feedback for the audience to feel listened to

Paint the picture to ensure others don't paint it for themselves

WHAT BREXIT DID

NO MANAGED CHANGE
- Focus has been on the struggle to Leave
- Little real world description of what the change will be for people and organisations
- Much left to the extremes of both sides to describe
LEAVE - wonderland
REMAIN - chaos

Seize the time... Live now! Make now always the most precious time. Now will never come again.
JEAN-LUC PICARD   Born 2305
Captain, USS Enterprise

MAKE IT HAPPEN
Change

People for Change

Use people to enable change

- ❏ Managers to support
  e.g. briefings to explain roadmap of change

- ❏ Influencers across the organisation to promote
  e.g. share early views of success

- ❏ External resources to demonstrate the future
  e.g. site visits to where changes are being used successfully, supplier demos

Keep it Simple

- ❏ People have crowded work lives so don't overwhelm them with complexity
  - ☒ They don't have the time to absorb your messages and fancy packaging!
  - ☒ They may start to see your change as hard work instead of exciting

- ❏ People may question how much is being spent on external consultants and an elaborate change programme
  - ☒ Especially when they may be struggling for Business As Usual resources themselves
  - ☒ Each time you add an additional component to your change programme, ask what extra value it will bring

- ❏ Focus on the message and keep the delivery simple — it will be really appreciated!

KOTTER

This standard widely recognised approach for change was designed by John P Kotter in 1995.

It focuses on 8 common errors and gives their antidote.

KOTTER Change Model

Establish a sense of urgency	Create the Guiding Coalition	Develop a Vision and a Strategy	Share the Change Vision	Empower Employees	Generate Short Term Wins	Consolidate Gains	Anchor New Approaches

WHAT BREXIT DID

Post Referendum, Leadership contest delays start	Hostile divisive debates in House of Commons	Slogans not Visions e.g. TAKE BACK CONTROL	No public information campaign until August 2019	No election No 2nd referendum	Blue cover back on passport	No publication of new trade deal progress	No shared plan for transition

MAKE IT HAPPEN
Quick Wins

A Quick Win is a small change that can be delivered early and demonstrate the benefits to be gained from the project as a whole.

Successful Quick Wins help build a good foundation for the rest of the project, gaining support and understanding.

❑ What are the options?

 ⌖ Brainstorm

 ⌖ Observe day-to-day work

 ⌖ Listen to suggestions

❑ What could be changed in the short term that could make a visible improvement?

❑ Where are most of the current issues?

❑ What would make most impact for the teams involved in the project?

❑ What is low risk to ensure success?

Ideas

❑ training opportunities

❑ improvements to the office environment

❑ improved processes

QUICK WINS
Many projects have long timelines which means waiting for the changes and benefits to materialise.
Quick wins create a momentum and demonstrate that the project is worth supporting.

But use Quick wins wisely.

There are pressures on leaders to provide quick wins, so don't fall or stumble trying to achieve early results. A project may obtain the outcome but at the expense of goodwill. If the process has been toxic the ability to inspire is undermined.

> You control your own wins and losses
>
> MARIA SHARAPOVA Born 1987
> Tennis player

WHAT BREXIT DID

NO IMMEDIATE BENEFITS
Claims that deal would be quick failed to happen
No one in charge of quick wins and demonstrating some immediate benefits
The day after we vote to leave, we hold all the cards and we can choose the path we want
Michael Gove April 2016

NEW PASSPORT COLOUR
Passport changed back to blue
- Symbolic but hollow gesture lost in bigger picture
- Ironically contract awarded to a French Company that was able to undercut UK providers prices

TRADE NEGOTIATIONS
No quick wins to indicate negotiation of new trade agreements was going well
Drowned by more interesting negatives largely created by media starved of real factual information.

Any positives were largely intangible.

N Negotiation

People have shades of opinion about the outcome and the best way to get there.   The key is finding consensus. Promote a feeling of being "invented here" to get people to be part of the solution.   This prevents the project stalling through indecision and disagreement as you go through the project.

• Know your Objective — what does success look like for you?

• What is their Objective — what does success look like for them?

There are at least two parties in a negotiation and often behind the negotiators there will be others they need to refer to or keep happy.   Think what their success or failure would look like.   e.g. unions with their members, employer with employees, the CEO with investors, suppliers with targets

Have a game plan beforehand but be prepared to be flexible. Find ideal positions, realistic positions and finally fall back positions.

You negotiate with humans not technology — after all the complex data on an Excel sheet a real human with emotions will make the decision !

Aim for WIN-WIN — face saving formulas or outcomes are definitely preferable. Imposed solutions are rarely as effective.

WHAT BREXIT DID

THERESA MAY &
BORIS JOHNSON
Repeated rejections of
deals and extensions to
EU exit as negotiations
have imposed solutions
without internal
negotiation.
Parliament as a whole
demanded input but also
failed to provide a single
agreed solution

Serious multilateral negotiating
experience is in short supply in
Whitehall, and that is not the case in
the [European] commission
or in the council.
SIR IVAN ROGERS Born 1960
Former UK Ambassador to EU

NEGOTIATION
Many views ... one vision

Humans make deals

Never underestimate the value of a good negotiating relationship.

- ❑ Know who you are negotiating with
    - ◄ read what you can online
      e.g. Linked In, blogs
    - ◄ use small talk
      e.g. breakfast meeting, coffee
- ❑ What is their default style?
    - ◄ Formal? Informal?
    - ◄ Competitive? Tough? Supportive?
    - ◄ Sensitive to reputation?
    - ◄ High or low expectations?
- ❑ How do they see the situation?
- ❑ What else is taking up their time and energy?

Make momentum

- ❑ Identify your "cabinet" to start to build a foundation of consensus
- ❑ Seek where most consensus can be found
    - ◄ Look for influencers to give you insights and speak on your behalf
    - ◄ Find where to gain a weight of numbers
    - ◄ Try to find some common ground for mutual dependency
    - ◄ Amass information and evidence to be shared across all negotiating parties
- ❑ Demonstrate understanding
- ❑ Be prepared to do deals with other areas indirectly impacted to develop a more organisation-wide mutually benefiting approach to change.

SECOND WORLD WAR
Many times BREXIT has been described as the biggest challenge since the Second World War.
So here's one of the things we did then ...
Churchill setup a cross party War Cabinet formed from
- Conservatives
- Labour
- Liberals

> Diplomacy is the art of letting someone else have your way
> SIR DAVID FROST 1939 – 2013
> Broadcaster

Consensus NOT Compromise

Theresa May failed to get consensus within her Cabinet to help build to her party and beyond

- Global
- EU
- UK public
- House of Commons
- Tory MPs
- Cabinet

WHAT BREXIT DID

MORE AND MORE VIEWS
Social and political disharmony
- In the House of Commons
- In board rooms
- In professional organisations, e.g. TUC, CBI etc..
- In families front rooms, pubs

High level of unfriending on Facebook !!

LACK OF CONSENSUS
- Negotiations driven by Theresa May's own Red Lines
- Her cabinet, party and rest of House of Commons alienated and their concerns ignored

UK and EU
- 27 countries to influence negotiations
- No identification of key influencers e.g. Leo Varadkar
- EU uses Theresa May's own words against her
Guy Verhofstadt
"Brexit deal requires strong & stable understanding"

NEGOTIATION
Deal or No Deal

Deal

- ❑ Collate background information in depth e.g. finances, head counts, projected costs, company performance, timeline, shareholder and stakeholder expectations

- ❑ Agree and brief your team with the key negotiation points
  - ⌐ Range of possible agreements
  - ⌐ Walk away point
  - ⌐ Worst alternative

- ❑ Find what you can give away without consequence of value to you but would have value for others

- ❑ Find a good mutually beneficial location e.g. agree to share hosting

- ❑ Never say NO immediately, always take some time to review and consider, then
  - ⌐ TRY *We considered that but after doing the numbers its a no*

- ❑ Share each consensus milestone as it is gained to create momentum of agreement

- ❑ Keep communication about the situation not about personalities.
  - TRY *I felt let down*
  - AVOID *You let me down*

No Deal

- ❑ Be prepared for where consensus is not possible and acknowledge that

- ❑ People can become entrenched in positions during negotiations and need to be focussed on why they are not moving position

- ❑ Don't make those that disagree with the consensus become enemies
  - ⌐ Offer them a constructive role
  - ⌐ Make it clear they matter by asking what is stopping them

- ❑ Try taking a break and reconvene

- ❑ When needed be prepare to walk away from negotiations to ensure you still will have a good agreement

Creativity not Conflict

PRINCIPLED NEGOTIATION
Fisher & Ury 1982
Focus for positive shared outcomes
- Set out what success would look like
- Look at alternatives to agreement
- Decide when you need to stop negotiations and use your BATNA

BATNA
Best Alternative To a Negotiated Agreement e.g build an extension instead of selling your house

WATNA
Worst Alternative To a Negotiated Agreement e.g. keep price too high

Duration and deadlines are key to negotiation strategy.

NO DEAL is Better Than a Bad Deal.
THERESA MAY Born 1956
Prime Minister

WHAT BREXIT DID

WATNA not BATNA
No Deal Better Than a Bad Deal
No Deal
- Only ever setup as WATNA
- NO DEAL loses advantage of preparation as not enough lead-time
- Time for organised managed exit with lead-time for efficient preparation

EU NEGOTIATION POINTS
- EU motivated to make a test case of UK to deter others
- Cracks in Government unity gave EU hope of reversing decision as in France, Ireland, and Denmark previously
- Member states vested interest
  Eire - Irish border
  Spain - Gibraltar

THERESA MAY
Theresa May undermined David Davis as Brexit minister
- no talk about consensus
- made arbitrary decisions and expect cabinet responsibility
- The Chequers deal led to resignations and discourse, mocked by political opponents and allies embarrassed

O Opinion

Many will have opinions about your project. Those within the project team and across the wider audience.

You need to be in control of your own message.

• Provide accurate and complete information

• Be ready to counter inaccurate and incomplete information

Some will have their own agendas. They may make it their mission to get a negative scoop on your project.   Unhelpful distractions need to be acknowledged and closed down with counter evidence.

Projects give a platform to launch and promote careers. Some will take every opportunity to take the stage and voice their opinion.

Make sure it's your opinion that is being heard, valued and trusted.

WHAT BREXIT DID

OPINION CHOICES ......
- BBC Reality Check
- SKY Opinion
- Legal Opinion
- EU Opinion
- Man on the Clapham Omnibus Opinion
- Former Prime Ministers Opinions
- Speakers Opinions
- Question Time Opinion
- Voted Out Opinion
- Voted Remain Opinion

There are as many opinions as there are experts
FRANKLIN D. ROOSEVELT 1882 – 1945
US President

OPINION
Fake News

Making the Fake News

What may be sources of fake news?

- ☐ Unintentional comments based on misunderstanding
- ☐ A soundbite to expose you and your project
- ☐ Loaded questions in meetings

Making your own Headlines

- ☐ Understand where influence is available and inform to right level
- ☐ Be prepared with counter information
- ☐ Be proactive in sharing information
- ☐ Welcome feedback to
  - ☐ control the message
  - ☐ expose behind the scenes comments as unhelpful

> **FALKLANDS WAR**
> Ian McDonald, Civil Service spokesman for the Ministry of Defence
> Factual
> Not emotive
> Seen as a success as a single trusted point of information

> ANON
> Unfortunately many of the third parties in Project BREXIT had an identity crisis! They never realised they were third parties.

UNTRUTH becomes TRUTH

WHAT BREXIT DID

EU MYTHS
- Curved bananas banned to prevent deformed bananas
- Prawn cocktail crisps banned by EU. It was a UK admin error
- Boris states EU require kippers to be kept cool in ice pillows for transit. A kipper is a smoked fish and so is not included.

NO CONTROL OF MESSAGE
UK Government has not consistently managed Brexit information,
- Leaflet before referendum
- Pubic information campaign from summer 2019
£350 million for NHS claim on campaign bus established a cynicism early in process

2019 BREXIT ELECTION
- Tory party rebadge their Twitter feed to appear as a Fact Checker source during the first leader debate
- Boris succeeds in message discipline within party "All 650 candidates back the deal"

OPINION

Outsiders

Some people will be involved specifically to give their opinion as experts. This may lead to their role becoming more and more dominant.

☐ Make it clear

- ☒ What you need from their expertise
- ☒ When you need an opinion
- ☒ When you need them to be involved in a decision

☐ Monitor their opinion and how it is being delivered

☐ Choose carefully and with full due diligence

**PESTON
ITV**

**KUENSSBERG
BBC**

**RIGBY
SKY NEWS**

Media Experts with increasing **high** profile and need to give insight.

WHAT BREXIT DID

MEDIA OPINIONS
- Intensive media coverage has often filled an information void, and made household names
- Some media outlets and individuals accused consistently of reporting bias
- Key individuals avoid key media outlets e.g. Jeremy Corbyn and Boris Johnson avoid Radio 4

OTHER OPINIONS
Gina Miller
- Clued up and full of certainty in comparison with government and opposition
- Giving instructions of how to vote for Remain in EU elections via own website
Anna Soubry
- Attracting counter-opinion of abusive nature

EU OPINION
- 27 governments one voice
- Very little contradiction given size of EU
- EU manage own internal dissent effectively e.g. Yellow Jackets, Catalan crisis, rising Nationalism

P - Planning

A project is a sequence of inter-related tasks. Time invested in planning the best sequence is invaluable in providing momentum and rhythm.

Your plan needs to recognise the dependencies that make up the backbone of your project. This creates a critical path of tasks to be monitored to ensure the overall timeline remains on track.

A good timeline or roadmap is clear to understand, and is shared to see how everyone's contribution impacts the successful delivery of the project.

People need to see the route to change clearly mapped out with stopping off points. Each stopping point should have a reason and be clear when to start again.

Also add milestones as key points of achievement. This creates momentum to be sustained through the project.

With a good plan you can forecast how long the project will take, and help to estimate resources and costs.

Plans are PLANs. They are a living document designed to be able to cope with change.

WHAT BREXIT DID

WHAT TO PLAN
Sir Jeremy Heywood, Cabinet Secretary & Head of the Civil Service to a committee of MPs: "We did, of course... in that last 28 days, look at what was being said by people advocating Leave and try to understand what were the issues that were likely to immediately arise on 24 June in that case."

Let our advance worries become our advance planning and thinking.
WINSTON CHURCHILL
1874 – 1965
Prime Minister

PLANNING
Top-Down, Bottom Up

Top-down

Begin with main headings, then the next levels, then the specifics

Bottom-up

Begin with specific tasks and decide what the main headings should be

Top-up

Combine the 2 approaches by having standard TOP headings and then build UP the detail from collaborative brainstorming

Structure

There are different ways to structure your plan

- ☐ By phases
- ☐ By deliverables
- ☐ Timeboxing

Sequence

- ☐ What tasks have fixed timings?
  e.g. new legislation begins
- ☐ Key time points to be worked around
  e.g. end of financial year, new software release, peak trading
- ☐ How are the tasks dependent on each other?
  - ⚅ Start is dependent on another Finishing
  - ⚅ Start is dependent on another Starting
  - ⚅ Finish is dependent on another Starting
  - ⚅ Finish is dependent on another being Finishing
  - ⚅ Can you run some tasks in parallel to reduce the timeline?
- ☐ Is there a Lead or Lag?
  - ⚅ Lead — start before the other task?
  - ⚅ Do you need to wait after another task to finish?
- ☐ How long each task will take?
  - ⚅ Is that fixed?
  - ⚅ Or faster with more people?
- ☐ Review to look at options for reducing the duration
  e.g. get more resource, less functionality, try parallel scheduling

CRITICAL PATH
Each project has a set of tasks with dependencies that create a critical path. This will determine the ultimate length of project. If any of these tasks are delayed the timeline of the project will increase.

MILESTONE
A milestone task is recorded with 0 duration. It represents an important achievement in a project.
e.g. approval, Go Live

Plans are worthless; planning is essential.
GENERAL EISENHOWER 1890 - 1961
US President

WHAT BREXIT DID

NO PLAN
Triggered Article 50 after increasing pressure from media, Parliament and interested parties (some then critical about Theresa May being hasty)
- without full discussion with cabinet
- without a negotiation plan
- without a roadmap to leaving
- without communication strategy

DIFFICULTIES TO COUNTER
Widely believed Civil Service and key civil servants were against Brexit
No-deal became a prominent spectre attracting negative speculation about food and medicine shortages.
Government failed to counter concerns.
Key people close to May not on message

MILESTONES
- Leaving date after Article 50
- A vote
- Another vote (meaningful)
- Another meaningful vote...
- Another leaving date
- EU MEP elections
- Another leaving date
- Another leaving date
- A General election
- Another leaving date

PLANNING
Make it Visual

THE AUDIENCE

Use the right tool to build, manage and share the plan with your audience.

Visuals

- Use post its to sequence tasks. Simply throw away when done.
POST ITs

| EU Referendum | Trigger Article 50 | Negotiate | Agree deal | Leave |

Roadmap

- Use graphics to show key milestones for presentations.
MS POWERPOINT SMARTART — Increasing Circle Process

EU Referendum   Trigger Article 50   Negotiate   Agree Deal   Leave

Gantt Charts

- Use Gannt Charts to manage more complex plans. These will include dependencies between tasks.
MICROSOFT PROJECT

	2016	2017	2018	2019	2020
EU Referendum	◆				
Trigger Article 50		◆			
Negotiate				↓ ↓	
Agree Deal				◆ ◆	
Leave					◆

PLANNING
The Long & Winding Roadmap

May 2015
- Cameron elected
- Starts EU re-negotiation

June 2016
- EU Referendum
- Cameron resigns

July 2016
- Theresa May becomes PM

Jan 2017
- Lancaster House speech BREXIT MEANS BREXIT

June 2018
- Withdrawal Bill becomes law

Dec 2017
- Divorce Bill agreed with backstop

June 2017
- General Election
- Tory majority lost

March 2017
- Article 50 triggered

July 2018
- Chequers followed by resignations

Nov 2018
- New withdrawal agreement – still with backstop

Dec 2018
- Pre Xmas vote on Deal cancelled

Jan 2019
- Meaningful Votes

May 2019
- Missed BREXIT deadline and extension agreed

May 2019
- EU elections

29 Mar 2019
- Missed BREXIT deadline and extension agreed

Mar 2019
- 21 Mar   Brussels 24 Mar Chequers

May 2019
- Theresa May resigns

July 2019
- Boris Johnson becomes PM

Aug 2019
- Parliament prorogued

Sep 2019
- MPs take control and prorogation reversed

Nov 2019
- BREXIT General Election called

Oct 31 2019
- Missed BREXIT deadline

19 Oct 2019
- "Super Saturday" in House of Commons

Oct 2019
- Johnson deal set out

12 Dec 2019
- General Election

31 Jan 2020
- Withdrawal Agreement passed

Transition Period to negotiate trade agreement

END ???

Q Question & Answers

Effective questioning plays an important part in projects.

The project team needs to ask questions to understand what is needed, and then to confirm how to best provide the right solution.

The stakeholders need to ask questions to confirm their understanding of the solution.

Good questioning skills need thought and puts the emphasis on the responses.

Additionally the project itself will be asked questions and need to have good responses.

WHAT BREXIT DID

HOUSE OF COMMONS Statements and positioning have become more important than forensic questioning of ministers
Public increasingly digests social media soundbites – not the detail, e.g. detailed Yellowhammer plans are distilled into 'disaster' headlines

Learn from yesterday, live for today, hope for tomorrow. The important thing is not to stop questioning
ALBERT EINSTEIN 1879 – 1955
Scientist

QUESTIONS & ANSWERS
Questioning

Open Questions

Encourage others to open up to give opinions and information.

- ❏ How do you feel about this project?
- ❏ What has worked well before?
- ❏ How would you sequence ... ?
- ❏ Why not?
- ❏ How would you go about it?
- ❏ How about looking at it from another viewpoint?

Closed Questions

Get a response to confirm specifics

- ❏ How many ...?
- ❏ How long ...?
- ❏ What are the best ..?
- ❏ When will ...?
- ❏ What is your name?

Getting the Flow

- ❏ Stay in control
  - ☐ Be prepared to be interrupted and side tracked
  - ☐ Do not rule out some detours if useful
- ❏ Balance talking with listening
- ❏ Allow thinking time
- ❏ Listen to replies
  - ☐ Do they sound confident or hesitant?
  - ☐ What can be inferred by what they are saying?
  - ☐ Does the tone of voice match what they are saying?
    e.g. stating support but sounding detached
- ❏ Observe and interpret non-verbal signals
  - ☐ Do they seem distracted? Why?
  - ☐ What are their facial expressions?
    e.g. smiles, raised eyebrows, head movements
  - ☐ What is their body language?
    e.g. folded arms, stabbing finger pointing, rolling eyes

BUILDING QUESTIONS
To what extent do you feel ...?
Just how far do you think ...?
In what ways ...?
To what degree ...?

SUPPORTING QUESTIONS
I see ...
That's interesting ...

REFLECTING QUESTIONS
You feel that ...
It seems to me that ...

> I am not responsible for what my face does when you talk
>
> UNKNOWN PUNK circa - 1977

WHAT BREXIT DID

TV and RADIO JOURNALISTS
- Often don't provide enough chance to answer before hitting with next question
- Interviewer and interviewee talking over each other
- Springing surprise questions unrelated to agreed topic
- Questions designed to lose face

AVOIDANCE
- many politicians avoiding answering the question asked WHY? now media trained, wised up to not make mistakes
- multiple choice questions with built in Yes or No leading to non-answers
- Use of questions designed to yield a juicy headline encourage avoidance techniques
e.g. just avoiding interviews

AVOIDANCE
High profile "interviews" away from political debate where easier to information to share and be digested.
- Holly and Phil, This Morning
- The One Show sofa
May 2019
Theresa May sparks controversy over who takes out the bins in the May household

QUESTION & ANSWERS
Answering

Having the Answer

- ❏ Look at each audience group
  - ⚊ What will they be likely to ask?
  - ⚊ What is their context and motivation for asking their questions?
- ❏ Brainstorm with the project team and key stakeholders to prepare your answers
- ❏ Construct the best responses
- ❏ Set up a project Frequently Asked Questions to agree consistent answers

ON MESSAGE

- ❏ Give one view from the project
- ❏ Reduce confusion and false information
- ❏ Draft and share standard responses across the team so there is consistency
- ❏ Keep key information and facts up to date and available for the team to use

Giving the Answer

- ❏ Embrace opportunities to answer questions
- ❏ Think about the tone and purpose of the questioner
  - ⚊ Is their motive clear?
  - ⚊ Take time with potentially loaded multiple choice and yes/no questions
  - ⚊ Be patient and assertive where the questioner is talking over you
- ❏ Think about the tone and purpose of your answer

reassuring confirming energising

- ❏ Keep it simple
  - ⚊ Use straightforward conversational language, free of jargon
  - ⚊ Most people just need and want the highlights
- ❏ Adapt answers for different audiences but always supply the same core truth

Always answer the ACTUAL question

WHAT BREXIT DID

LABOUR PARTY
- Multiple versions of responses to the same question in different interviews
- Over complex responses

MEDIA DEBATES
- Theresa May sends in Amber Rudd to 2017 Leaders debate
- Increasing use of politicians using social media to soundbite answers
- Desperate mediators and over assertive participants lead to answers being talked over

FAILURE OF FACTS
- BBC Question Time audience more and more unhappy about politicians not answering questions asked
- Conveyor belt of politicians from all sides not having as many facts as Andrew Neil
- More concerned with saving face - themselves or party, than answering question

R Risks & Issues

Very few changes come without risk or issues to deal with.

- Risks MAY happen and impact the project
- Issues ARE happening and are already impacting the project

Projects have problems, and these will disrupt the project. How well cope with risk issues is a major way projects succeed or fail.

WHAT BREXIT DID

NOT IDENTIFYING
RISKS
- Failed to anticipate
something fundamental
i.e. the referendum
might give. an outcome
of *LEAVE*
Failed to anticipate
societal schism and
evolving grievance
both sides perceived

The biggest risk is
not taking any risk...
In a world that's changing really
quickly, the only strategy that is
guaranteed to fail is not taking risks.
MARK ZUCKERBERG   Born 1984
Founder, Facebook

RISKS & ISSUES
A Risky Business

identifying
- ☐ High level look for risks to evaluate feasibility
- ☐ Work more detail for the business case
- ☐ Review and manage throughout the project

Assessing
Look at each risk to find its risk factor
- ☐ How likely is the risk to become an issue?
  High – less 10%
  Medium – 10-30%
  Low – more than 30%
- ☐ How would the project be impacted?
  - ◾ Extends time
  - ◾ Increases cost
  - ◾ Restrict outcome
  Large/moderate/small

Likelihood

+ ➡ Overall risk

Impact

Managing
- ☐ Agree an owner
- ☐ Agree the actions to be taken for each risk

AVOID
- If possible, reduce the likelihood as low as possible

MITIGATE
- When AVOID is not possible
- Reduce impact

TRANSFER
- Shift impact to somewhere else
- e.g. take insurance

ACCEPT
- When other actions are more costly or damaging than the potential impact

> When you take risks you learn that there will be times when you succeed and there will be times when you fail, and both are equally important.
> ELLEN DEGENERES Born 1958
> US broadcaster

WHAT BREXIT DID

NO DEAL ... NO RISK?
Risk of NO DEAL not managed, in fact some sectors seemed to welcome a no deal Brexit with WTO rules CBI and George Osborne warnings of immediate emergency budget and economic/employment impact never materialised consequently follow up warnings dismissed as similarly not credible.

PROJECT FEAR & FAKE NEWS
No shortage of top 10 risks
- Shopping basket will change
- Increased gas and electric rates
- Drug shortage
- Travel issues abroad
- Delays at ports and motorways
- House price impact (up and down)

RISK OF EXTENSIONS
- Risk of final crash out
- Benefit of WTO and final crash out
- Continued uncertainty impacts pound and business
- Public become increasingly frustrated and fatigued
- Investment in UK cancelled or delayed or moved
- Risk of instability in EU

RISKS & ISSUES
Issues

Identify

☐ What is already affecting the project?

☐ How is it affecting the project?

☐ What is the level of the impact?

Manage

☐ Can actions be taken to manage the impact, or address the issue itself?

☐ What is the cost of resolving the issue?

☐ How significantly does that impact the overall benefits ?

☐ If actions are agreed agree an owner to manage the reduction or resolution of impact

Issue priority

Which issue is the most urgent? What should be prioitised?

☐ Immediate

☐ Soon

☐ Later

Issue severity

How bad the consequence would be if the issue is left unsolved?

☐ Major

☐ Medium

☐ Minor

> APOLLO 13
> Houston we have a problem

WHAT BREXIT DID

RISKS & OPPORTUNITIES
- 95% of Companies mention Brexit in annual report
- NHS loses people resources
- Economical to Taxation and Foreign Exchange
- NFU warn bad for Farmers

HOUSE OF COMMONS
Issue not resolved
- EU Referendum vote to Leave
- Majority in House of Commons are Remainers; some representing Leave constituency but large majority voted to honour referendum vote
- 2019 Election resolves issue by giving Boris Johnson the majority to pass the deal in the Commons

UNINTENDED COSEQUENCES Health and safety / Wellbeing
- Long hours in chamber
- Holidays cancelled
- Robust and vigorous exchanges in Parliament
- Robust and vigorous changes outside Parliament
- Accusations of bullying and threats
- Wellbeing of some MP's

S Solution

Many projects start with a solution without investing time in assessing what their real requirements are — what they NEED.   Gathered from different perspectives.   Once you know the requirements you can start to look for the best solution. Requirements are the criteria for selecting the solution that best fits.

Takes time, skill and effort

- Too long may compromise how much they truly reflect a changing organisation, and also increase the overall time of the project

- Not long enough may compromise the quality of the requirements

Get the requirements right

- represent different viewpoints

- the longer a wrong requirement is included, the more it will cost the project in time and money.

The requirements must be practical, achievable and add value.

Keep asking WHY not WHAT and HOW

With a good set of requirements you know what your need is, and then you can start looking for the right solution.

WHAT BREXIT DID

Focus on in or out of EU without detailed requirements of what voters wanted
No realistic information on how Brexit would impact voters daily lives
No apparent plan to provide either of the above and proposed solutions
– But life carried on!

Identify your problems but give your power and energy to solutions.
ANON

SOLUTION

Requirements are Not the Solution ...

What needs to be different?

Identify the key requirements that will MAKE the change happen

- What will add value?
  Functional – What does it need to do?
  Non Functional – How well does it need to work?

- Involve all impacted but have a clear arbitrator to agree the consensus view

- Invest time to provide background information to help fill gaps of knowledge and experience

- Set up an environment where all can talk openly

  - Ensure balance with day job to give time to think

  - Plan a mix of 1:1s, workshops and workplace visits

  - Facilitate group sessions for everyone to be heard

  - Make it interesting to contribute e.g. brainstorms, visual boards, show and tell, site visits

- What do competitors do?

Are they the right requirements?

- How do they fit together?
  - Conflicting?
  - Contradictory?
- Prioritise
  - Identify how each fit with strategic goals
  - Look at the value added directly or to enable other requirements

MOSCOW PRIORITISATION

MUST
- Needed for the objectives to be met

SHOULD
- Need to meet full potential of objective

COULD
- Not needed to achieve the end objective, but will support

WON'T
- Not needed as Inconsistent/unnecessary to achieve the end objective

WHAT BREXIT DID

BORDER SOLUTION
Government faced with needing solution for Ireland border satisfactory to DUP and Eire.
- EU provide one (solution) which creates border down Irish sea.
- Technology solution dismissed by EU and dropped (rather quickly)

THERESA MAY'S RED LINES
- European Court of Justice
- No to the Customs Union
- No to free movement
- No EU budget contributions after the Divorce Bill
- An EU official described May's opening agenda for talks as an eye-opener.
- "It felt to the EU side like she does not live on planet Mars but rather in a galaxy very far away."

LABOUR'S 6 TESTS
1. Does it ensure a strong and collaborative future relationship with the EU?
2. Does it deliver the "exact same benefits" as we currently have as members of the Single Market and Customs Union?
3. Does it ensure the fair management of migration in the interests of the economy and communities?
4. Does it defend rights and protections and prevent a race to the bottom?
5. Does it protect national security and our capacity to tackle cross-border crime?
6. Does it deliver for all regions and nations of the UK?

SOLUTION
The End Game

Once the requirements have been agreed, you need to find a solution that will reflect the requirements best.

❑ Agree how to choose the best solution
  - What is the most important?
  - Relative weight of criteria

❑ Setup Q&A sessions for people to share views and information

❑ Ask how the solution might be tested before finally agreed

❑ Make sure any terminology or jargon is understood by providing a glossary

❑ Review of each option

❑ A description and evaluation of the best option

❑ Showcase examples and prototypes

If it looked like this would it meet your needs?

❑ What are the Issues and assumptions?

❑ What are the risks?

❑ What is the value to customers?

❑ How easy to deliver?

❑ Has anyone done this before?

How to compare?

Focus on evaluating solutions and making a decision. Determine relative weighting of criteria to reflect what is important to the outcome.

❑ Only spend time on real hopes

❑ Ease of application — how simple to deliver?

❑ What are the risks?

❑ How disruptive to business?

❑ What are the financials?
  e.g. NPV, IRR, payback period

❑ How long do tasks take to complete?

❑ How accurate is the output?

❑ How much training is needed to get to a level of proficiency?

❑ What do users say about it?

❑ How long is training remembered?

REQUIREMENT
Increase the control in decision making between the UK and the EU

SOLUTIONS		
REMAIN	LEAVE No Deal	LEAVE With a Deal

GEORGE BRIDGES Former Parliamentary Under-Secretary of State for Exiting the European Union

WHAT BREXIT DID

- No signed off LEAVE requirements before referendum so no clear solution
- Nigel Farage initially rejects Boris Johnson deal as only BREXIT in name
- Lots of debate and controversy about Irish border without focus on detail of a solution
- But the border in the sea came back as an option

Yes, white papers were published, but behind them lay fuzzy thinking.
The opaque description for our objective was a 'bespoke partnership'. Bespoke means tailored for the individual.
To Remainers one could say: 'Yes, Dominic, we will continue to have frictionless trade — suits you sir!'
To Brexiteers: 'Don't worry, Iain, we've seen the back of those EU judges — suits you sir!'

T Team

Each project needs to have the right blend of behaviours, processes and governance.

There are common features for most projects to get a motivated team producing great well received results.

• Acknowledged leadership

• Clarity of purpose

• Trust in each other's abilities

A good team is a mix of talents, experience and opinions.   The team is made of individuals but will function as the sum of the parts.   Make room for big personalities but every team has only one leader.

The better the team building, the best chance of keeping the team intact to provide continuity.

Build a team with right skills, competencies and culture.

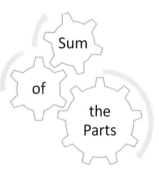

WHAT BREXIT DID

THERESA MAY
- appointed her cabinet and then did it all herself
- team quickly became dysfunctional without respect leading to several reshuffles
- attempted to reach out with cross party to build a wider team but too late

Leaders instil in their people a hope for success and a belief in themselves. Positive leaders empower people to accomplish their goals.
ANON

TEAM

The Dream Team

Build

- [ ] Building a project team with clear roles and responsibilities but able to cross skill and support each other when required
- [ ] In addition, include all those touched by the project as feeling part of a wider team
- [ ] The skills, experience and knowledge of the team is the cornerstone of the project
- [ ] The use of external resources can be controversial and needs to be carefully managed
- [ ] Look at power and influence
  - Seniority
    e.g. senior managers making decisions without enough understanding
  - Knowledge
    e.g. Compliance, Finance, IT

How

- [ ] Take time to see who is available, including external options
- [ ] Get mix of internal and external resources right
- [ ] Mix opinions and styles
- [ ] Value and acknowledge professionalism
- [ ] Communicate
  - Choose good collaborative tools e.g. Trello
  - Use offsite days when need to focus
- [ ] Acknowledge personal perspectives

BELBIN

Belbin's 1981 book Management Teams presented conclusions from his work studying how members of teams interacted during business games run at Henley Management College.

The observations include 9 key roles to function effectively as a team.

BELBIN TEAM ROLES

Action oriented roles	People oriented roles	Cerebral roles
•Shaper	•Co-Ordinator	•Plant
•Implementer	•Team worker	•Monitor Evaluator
•Completer Finisher	•Resource Investigator	•Specialist

WHAT BREXIT DID

NEGOTIATING SKILLS
EU have experienced team of trade negotiators
UK had none
- role no longer required in UK as EU had carried out our trade negotiations
- Increased skills developing but lack of alternatives makes for a lack of bargaining power in team

ADVISERS
Sonia Khan, Sajid Javid's media adviser
- escorted from No 10 by a police officer as Dominic Cummings believed in touch with group trying to block a NO DEAL
- Tory anger at Cummings role in purge of Brexit rebels

THERESA'S INNER CIRCLE
Fiona Hill & Nick Timothy, advisers to Theresa May
- undermined cabinet team
- replaced after 2017 election
- Ministers could not get to May unless through them
Seen to be working with civil servants more than her BREXIT secretaries

TEAM
Continuity

- ❏ A new CEO with changed senior leadership team
- ❏ A new project manager
- ❏ A new technical lead
- ❏ Key business resources, experts and influencers

- ❏ Wastes time of project and business
- ❏ Gives poor external view

What can you do?
- ❏ Formal
  - ⌐ Review notice periods
  - ⌐ Where possible, use permanent resources
  - ⌐ Place a value on the need for continuity by offering retention incentives
- ❏ Informal
  - ⌐ Documentation
  - ⌐ Talk to the team
  - ⌐ Accommodate

LARRY THE CAT
Providing continuity
at No 10

WHAT BREXIT DID

2018
25 cabinet resignation
1st half 2019
14 cabinet resignations
2nd half 2019
- Reduced resignations
- Cabinet stability
- Government succeeds in getting Withdrawal Agreement through Parliament

Prime Ministers

David Cameron
- 11/05/2010 13/07/2016

➡

Theresa May
- 13/07/2016-24/07/2019

➡

Boris Johnson
- 24/07/2019-Incumbent

David Davis
13/07/2016 – 18/09/2017

➡

Dominic Raab
09/07/2018 – 15/11/2018

➡

BREXIT Secretaries

Stephen Barclay
16/11/2018
incumbent

U The Unknown

Projects rarely stay on track as planned.   There will be changes.

Some changes will have been thought about as possibilities; others will remain unknown until they happen.

Reduce the number of unknowns by thinking about internal and external changes that may impact the plan.

Be prepared for the unknown. It is part of managing a project.   Having effective contingency plans are the skill of managing the potential impact of risks.   You can then react faster by having a contingency plan.

The contingency needs to be appropriate to risk — its likelihood and impact.

You also need a general contingency of time and budget for unplanned unknowns.

There are some things you do know.   These are assumptions that look like certainties to base decisions on — your KNOWN KNOWNs.

WHAT BREXIT DID

REMAIN PREDICTIONS
Based on the referendum Leave result but never materialised
- downturn in the economy
- loss of 500k jobs
- immediate £20billion emergency budget in the days following Yes, and 6 months for loss of jobs
So Brexiteers able to constantly question unknowns.

There are known knowns; there are things we know we know. We also know there are known unknowns; that is to say we know there are some things we do not know.
DONALD RUMSFELD   Born 1932
US politician

THE UNKNOWN
Known Knowns

Assuming the assumptions

- ❏ Statements to describe events or statuses that are expected to be true during the project
- ❏ Based on experience or evidence from data
- ❏ Review and test through the lifetime of the project
- ❏ Assess likelihood of assumption being false
- ❏ Assess impact and risk
- ❏ Share and confirm with all
- ❏ Reasonable to make assumption?
- ❏ Validate formally with stakeholders

What you know

95% staff will move to the new office location

UK economic growth will remain at 3% during project life cycle.

Make the Unknown Known

You must stick to your conviction, but be ready to abandon your assumptions.
DENIS WAITLEY   Born 1933
Motivational speaker

WHAT BREXIT DID

ISLAND OF IRELAND
- Irish border solution needs to uphold internationally ratified Good Friday Agreement
- Ireland ready to absorb impact of NO DEAL with 1.2billion euro fund
- UK reiterates will not put up hard border, meaning Ireland may have to

REMAIN ASSUMPTIONS
- Leave result of EU Referendum will start a recession
- Mass exodus of businesses to Europe, Paris and Frankfurt for financial institutions
- No investment in UK
- Skilled EU workforce will leave
- Northern Ireland peace at risk
- Families will be financially worse off

BREXITEER ASSUMPTIONS
- Leaving negotiations will be easy
- EU needs to maintain integrity of Union but will do a deal
- EU needs us more than we need EU so they will do a deal
- Trade deals will be easy to do with rest of world

THE UNKNOWN
Plan B

- ❏ Be prepared for the Unknown,
- ❏ Look at
  - ⊌ each risk, identifying what would have to be put in place if happened
  - ⊌ each dependency, identifying what would happen if did not happen?
- ❏ Set contingencies in the plan and budget
- ❏ Review regularly
  - ⊌ What contingencies neede
  - ⊌ Have costs risen for the ic contingencies?
- ❏ Unknowns
  - ⊌ Need to be able to deploy in time
  - ⊌ How much money and tim allocated to contingencies

  - ⊌ Get everyone to look for v contingency plans may be

> Sometimes good things fall apart so better things can fall better
> MARILYN MONROE   1926 — 1962
> Actress and icon

Dominic Grieve — one of the Parliamentarians with interventions to the plans of Theresa May and Boris Johnson.

WHAT BREXIT DID

HOUSE OF COMMONS
Interventions that have needed a contingency plan e.g. Dominic Grieve
No contingency for Parliament being at odds with electorate and how to address
No cross party consensus despite call from all parties for cross party talks

NO DEAL IS BETTER THAN A BAD DEAL
- Is this a contingency?
- Is this planning for failure?
Approach leads to delay and lack of direction for NO DEAL planning
- No cost:benefits analysis e.g. booking of ferry companies, refrigerated storage to stockpile medical supplies

PROJECT YELLOW HAMMER
Contingency planning for the UK leaving with NO DEAL developed by the Civil Contingencies Secretariat
- Money spent on preparation for NO DEAL acknowledging 31 March as dependency
- Wasted money and resource as no lead time to NO DEAL agreed and then date extended

V Value

Projects exist to add value to your customers, providing a product or service that includes features they will really value.

Projects exist to add value to your organisation, by making money or saving enough money to significantly offset the costs

- By reducing costs
- By avoiding costs
- By increasing revenue
- By helping and supporting organisation goals

Benefits don't just happen if the project is completed.   You need to plan in how they will continue to add value after the project has formally ended.

A benefit cannot be of value if it cannot be achieved.

VALUE
Visioning the Value

Find the Value

- ❏ Identify the benefits that will support your organisation's urgent business strategy and Key Performance Indicators
- ❏ Quantify using Best-Most Likely-Worst scenarios
  - ▪ Will the benefits be felt the same across the organization?
  - ▪ Which benefits/costs have a high impact?
    i.e.. Change small %, impact high %
- ❏ Use an objective resource combining financial analysis skills with commercial and people view to review and feedback

Plan & Track

- ▪ Embed benefits tracking and success in the project timeline
- ❏ Test through the project to adjust if needed
- ❏ Include benefits review in all project changes
  - ▪ Is there now a higher/lower risk that the benefits can be achieved?
  - ▪ Have the assumptions proved accurate?
  - ▪ How are external factors impacting your benefits expectations? e.g. economic climate, sector trends

Why?

- ❏ Give upfront tests for when to stop a project if costs outweigh benefits
- ❏ Demonstrates accountability
- ❏ Increase confidence of investors and funders
- ❏ As part of continuous improvements from learning what works

What are the Tangible Benefits?
- • This is value that can be seen as profit and loss.
  e.g. Revenue, cost reductions, cost avoidance, organisation's financial approach

What are the Intangible Benefits?
- • This is the value felt by customers and employees.
  e.g. Trustpilot scores, staff satisfaction, complaint levels, investor confidence, employee skills and experience, reduced risks

Measure all projects the same way

How accurate is the forecast?

WHAT BREXIT DID

FREEDOM FROM EU
Leave campaign appealed to ingrained sense UK can look after itself
- Perception that EU extending powers
e.g. Dec 2011 David Cameron vetoes the EU finance treaty on euro, which EU then ignores

ACCESS TO WORLD TRADE
Leave campaign promote that the UK can do better deals around the world
- Feeling that EU protectionism stifling opportunities

IMMIGRATION
Perceived threat of increased migrant flows
Aug 2015
Germany unilaterally abandons Dublin regulation for determining responsibility for those seeking asylum. Tries to persuade other states to do same.

VALUE
Valuing Value

Include a benefits champion in the team to challenge and monitor progress of benefits

☐ Set expected overall benefits at the start

☐ Monitor and confirm throughout with adjustments for changes

☐ As important in the middle, end and post project as at the start

Some benefits are tangible and can be measured; others are intangible and cannot be measured.

Features & Benefits

☐ Focus on the value given by the benefits — not the features

  ☑ A system with a faster processing feature does not add value

  ☑ Processing orders faster for customer delivery does add value

☐ Could time and effort provide more value being used elsewhere?
NOTE — this may include investing it financially and not in funding a project

> A man who knows the price of everything and the value of nothing
> OSCAR WILDE   1854 – 1900
> Playwright and author

WHAT BREXIT DID

INTANGIBLE
Too much emphasis on intangible
Britain better bet for trade and investment than from being in the EU. This could not be proved, always a forecast.
But still it did not matter....

BREXIT
- Freedom
- Unshackled
- Control
- Cost saving as a benefit
- Some of the EU contribution would still be used to fund initiatives in the UK

EU PREPARES POST BREXIT
- When UK gone so is the distraction
- EU knows now it must reform itself, particularly the euro, soft exit for some countries, develop sensible strategy re migration
- Review the rate of integration and let it evolve
- New dynamic economic growth

W Ways of Working

Project teams are at the forefront of creating opportunities to make organisations more efficient and innovative.   This maybe a new IT system, new office facilities or a merger with another organisation.

Project teams should demonstrate

- Great collaboration across teams
- Adoption of new innovative efficient tools and techniques

And they should be ready to share these improvements with others.

Some will be standard ways of working like effective time management; others will be demonstrating innovative ways of running projects like working in an Agile approach.

WHAT BREXIT DID

Parliament still have traditional ways of working
- Late night sittings
- Long holidays
Brexit brought power of social media to the front bench's, back benches, Lords and other institutions
- When Parliament wanted to block Government proroguing managed it in a couple of days – amazing
- The Benn Act regarding extension

WAYS OF WORKING
Creating WOWs

Setup for Success

☐ Launch the project with agreed Ways of Working that will suit the project e.g. flexible working, remote working

☐ Get ideas from across the project team of how to work effectively

  ⊟ How have they worked on other projects?

  ⊟ What do they think might be useful for this project?

☐ Be clear on only doing activities that add real value to the outcome, avoiding "tick box" tasks

Lead by Example

☐ The project team Ways of Working can be a vital part of the project itself e.g. A digital transformational project needs to demonstrate and fully utilise digital tools and techniques themselves

☐ Actively promote and demonstrate innovative tools and techniques

☐ Everyone needs to feel inspired by how the project team is working

Business As Usual

Take time to understand how the teams work in their normal routine outside the project.

☐ What are the key events in the business year? e.g. peak trading, end of financial year, holiday times

☐ How do people work? e.g. home working

Live the Project!

> I'm interested in things that change the world or that affect the future and wondrous, new technology where you see it, and you're like, 'Wow, how did that even happen? How is that possible?'
> ELON MUSK Born 1971
> Entrepreneur

WHAT BREXIT DID

TECHNOLOGY
- Not enough focus on using technology
e.g. solutions for Irish border
- Technology as means of communication

NO UK WOW FACTOR
- Bemusement round the world as UK viewed as floundering and illogical
- Parliament dysfunctional and split
- Within UK public whether remain or leave frustrated at lack of progress
- Not an inspiring process to build brave new world

TACTICAL VOTING
- Most thought and effort focussed on thwarting Brexit instead of creating effective WOWs
- Open calls to vote tactically in general election to stop Brexit
- Second referendum result – 1-1 or 2-0, 1-1 will merely prompt best of 3

WAYS OF WORKING
Work Smarter not Harder

Time

- ☐ Prioritise tasks by urgency and importance as work arrives
  - ☒ Urgency — when needs to be completed?
  - ☒ Important — what happens if not done?
  - ☒ What needs to be worked on with others?
- ☐ Zone your day
  - ☒ Review emails
  - ☒ Write reports and documents
- ☐ Expect new unknown work to arrive during each day
- ☐ Don't overwork and over analyse — only do what will add value
- ☐ Better to say no than disappoint with non delivery or poor quality

Work Visually

- ☐ Have walls displaying project plan, current work from the project
- ☐ Draw storyboards to help understand how things work

Collaboration

- ☐ Share information in ways that mirror the aim of the project itself e.g. digital tools
- ☐ Run effective focussed meetings
  - ☒ Have a clear agenda/objectives
  - ☒ Run as a stand up to keep pace and momentum
  - ☒ It is needed? Even if a regularly scheduled meeting

Learn Learn Learn

- ☐ Look for new tools and techniques that can help the project
- ☐ Share knowledge and experience

SAYING NO

Try to offer alternatives

"No but what we can do ..."

"No but how about ..."

Give some context

"Friday is the team's busiest day ..."

It is the long history of humankind (and animal kind, too) that those who learned to collaborate and improvise most effectively have prevailed. CHARLES DARWIN — 1809 - 1882 Scientist

---

WHAT BREXIT DID

STAGGER NOT SPRINT
- No feeling of urgency with milestones on way to bigger deadlines even with the Genie out of the Bottle
- Lulls in activity and then flurry to meet a deadline – which passes
- Still appears that there is no end to Project Brexit

MISSED DEADLINES
March 29 2019
April 12 2019
October 31 2019 - Halloween
Die in a ditch quote from PM – apologises for missing deadline

EU grants extensions
Next date Jan 31 2020 !!

BREXIT LEARNING – ALL
- No-one gets out of this process looking good
- The future belongs to the learners not the Right Honourable learned
- Remain and Leave campaigns – both exaggerated
- EU direct democracy v representative democracy Is Brexit a warning not to take the electorate for granted?

WAYS OF WORKING
Making Time

Run a TO DO list by prioritising tasks looking at urgency and importance.

DO FIRST

- Tasks to be done today (tomorrow at latest)

SCHEDULE

- Tasks to de done but not today
- Where most tasks sit

DELEGATE

- Tasks to be done today/soon but not necessarily by you

DON'T DO

- Its not urgent or important
- Don't do it unless you have spare time

	URGENT	NOT URGENT
	DO FIRST	**SCHEDULE**
IMPORTANT	crisis point/project deadlines e.g. review report for board meeting next day	preparation/planning/relationship building
	DELEGATE	**DON'T DO**
NOT IMPORTANT	at desk interruptions, some emails/calls/messaging e.g. ad hoc advice suggest an alternative	timewasters, general emails/calls/messaging/meetings e.g. regular meeting you attend but only valid for 5 mins

That's been one of my mantras - focus and simplicity. Simple can be harder than complex: You have to work hard to get your thinking clean to make it simple. But it's worth it in the end because once you get there, you can move mountains.
STEVE JOBS   1955 – 2011
Co-founder Apple

X   Project X

Project X represents the projects and parts of projects subject to confidentiality.

• Critical information being leaked can sideline or even stop a project.

It is important to be practical — think about how being confidential looks to the rest of the organisation.

Make sure confidentiality is truly confidential and everyone knows why.   Not just to make the project team feel even more important.

Leaks may happen accidently or intentionally, but these can cost projects.

Private might be useful; secretive is deceptive.

PROJECT X
Keeping it in the Team

Controlling the pace information is shared controls the message. This can encourage a project team to be secretive due to control a real need for confidentiality.

What's a Secret?

❑ Be practical and think through what really needs to be kept confidential

- ▪ Will concealing it prevent progress?
- ▪ Will concealing it prevent the team making the best decisions?
- ▪ Will concealing it make people anxious by filling in the gaps?

Who knows?

❑ Look for loopholes e.g.IT support

❑ Be consistent – include new people and third parties

❑ Look for unintentional places to leak

❑ Controlled communication lowers the risk of leaks

Working in Secret

❑ Get the right space to allow for discussions in confidence

- ▪ walls have ears; meeting rooms can have thin walls
- ▪ if you need to work in a designated area choose somewhere discrete - do not make a drama out of it being confidential.

❑ Use NDAs (Non Disclosure Agreements) to manage risks of confidential information being leaked

❑ Open organisations are an aspiration — difficult in reality.

> The key to business is differentiation, then speed to market, your differentiation will be copied courtesy of the internet in hours. So be discreet before it even gets there
> P***** off CEO
> ANON

WHAT BREXIT DID

LEAKS not OPEN GOVERNMENT
- Cabinet leaks
e.g. unnamed sources to media
- Civil Service leaks
e.g. Dec 2019 Leaked Treasury analysis of impact on Northern Ireland for the new Boris Johnson deal
- Parliament and Court force Government to share more

NEGOTIATIONS
Keeping negotiation secret
MAY
- result comes as a surprise
BORIS
- people question whether there are any negotiations

ANDREA LEADSOM
- MPs vote for publication of Yellowhammer document
- Andrea Leadsom says the NO DEAL predictions were too scary for public
- Already leaked in The Sunday Times warns of food shortages, long border queues & civil unrest

PROJECT X
Loose Talk

There are opportunities for information to be leaked.

By mistake

❑ **People**

- ☒ Some people cannot stop sharing information even when they have been told not to
- ☒ Others are not very careful about where they talk
- ☒ No password management

❑ **Physical mistakes**

- ☒ Paperwork not shredded
- ☒ Memory sticks misplaced
- ☒ Mislaid laptops
- ☒ Meeting briefs visible to photographers

With intent

❑ **Whistle-blowers**

- ☒ Leaks are often associated with things not working and people feel the need to share outside the project team.
- ☒ Be proactive and control the message. Ensure you include about any problems what is being done to manage them.

❑ **Commercial advantage**

- ☒ Use NDAs to formally protect commercial information

WHAT BREXIT DID

COVER UP YOUR PAPERS
- Notice on door of no 10
- Government failed to manage media, judiciary became involved and also individuals bringing court actions on non-legal matters – forcing more open government
- Judges perceived to be involving themselves in non legal matters

- May clumsily attempted to lay down expectation at start saying would not update daily
- Provoked press and opposition
- Public feels their Human Right to know !

LEAKS
- Philip Hammond tweets letter explaining why he and other former ministers are not the leakers of the YellowHammer dossier
- Leaked Whitehall briefings
- NO DEAL dossier perceived to have been used selectively

Y You

YOU may play different roles in projects over time.

- Lead a project
- Contribute directly to a project
- Adapt to changes and impacts from a project
- Receive new products and services as a customer

Use these experiences to empathise and help support others

- Lead with the respect you would like to experience
- Communicate issues about your contributions early and constructively
- Be open to change, looking for ways to maximise value for you and your customers

In any role, you can contribute more by harnessing your emotional intelligence factoring in feeling as well as rational analysis.

- Understand your own emotions
- Raise your awareness of the emotions of others

In all cases using empathy will enable projects to deliver great results in a collaborative and creative way.

WHAT BREXIT DID

LACK OF EMPATHY
Politicians and public alike have showed little interest in seeing other's view points.
- Debates in Parliament, on TV and Social Media very emotional
- Calls for calm from all sides of the debate

If you see someone without a smile, give them one of yours.
DOLLY PARTON   Born 1946
Singer and Songwriter

YOU
And everyone else

Being emotionally intelligent

Harnessing the benefits of emotional intelligence is a key differentiator that provides:

❑ Effective collaboration across teams

❑ Reduced causes and impacts of stress

❑ Better understanding of your customers

 Self Awareness
- Acknowledge your own feelings
- Know what you value & care about
- Recognise the rules to live by

 Social Awareness
- Use empathy to feel how it is to walk in someone else's shoes
- Understand the emotions, needs and concerns of others
- Recognise emotional cues

 Self Management
- Control impulsive unproductive behaviours
- Step back and choose how to react
- Adjust your emotions, thoughts and behaviour to changing situations

 Relationship Management
- Develop and maintain productive relationships
- Communicate clearly, tailored to the receiver
- Inspire and influence others, contribute positively to a team

 Stress Management
- Find ways that suit you to deal with stressful situations
- Get into the habit of having a positive attitude, even in adverse conditions
- Consider your own Well-being and that of the team

EMOTIONAL INTELLIGENCE
Defined by Peter Salowy and John D Mayer in 1990, then popularised by Daniel Goleman in 1998.
Followed by Reuven Bar-On in 2000 with Emotional Quotient Inventory (EQI)

Understand, use and manage your own emotions positively.
- Relieve stress
- Communicate effectively
- Empathise with others
- Overcome challenges
- Defuse conflict

Health is a state of complete physical, mental and social well-being, and not merely the absence of disease or infirmity.
WORLD HEALTH ORGANISATION

WHAT BREXIT DID

EMOTIONS
SEPT 2019
House of Commons confrontational debates without end in sight hitting a low in September 2019 with little control of personal emotions
- Claims and counter claims of bullying
- Jeremy Hunt compares EU to Soviet Union

ASSERTIVE v AGGRESSIVE
- Communication style in the House of Commons and with media has been aggressive rather than assertive.
- Claims and counter claims of blame from 'Traitorous' Remainers and 'Lying' Brexiters
- Out campaign accuses EU of following path f Napoleon trying to create superstate

ADAPTABILITY
- Many Remainers have not been able to adjust to the reality of the outcome of the referendum
- Merkel warns both EU and UK against rigid approach to talks

Z Zeitgeist

Zeitgeist is the defining spirit or mood of a particular period of history demonstrated by ideas and beliefs.

Projects offer an escape - a much more interesting distraction from the usual day job. People may also find themselves with a sense of power and importance they may not have had before.

So all too easily a project team form a world of their own. Spending more time with each other, and less time with the people they are working for.

The project team then becomes cut off from the zeitgeist.

Understanding and using the zeitgeist is key to real support for your project. It helps to communicate in the right way and about the things the audience really care about.

Without getting the zeitgeist the project works inside its own bubble, talking about things that are not of much concern outside the project.

It is harder to sell keeping the status quo if the change is compelling and sounds exciting.

Some projects should be communicated in a plain, simple, practical way. Others need to be communicated as a marketing campaign to create energy and interest, and to generate cultural transition.

WHAT BREXIT DID

DANNY DYER
June 2018
"Who knows about Brexit? No one has got a f****** clue what Brexit is, yeah. You watch Question Time, it's comedy. No one knows what it is – it's like this mad riddle that no one knows what it is, right?"
By October 2019
Proven descendant of royalty, his own prime time Saturday night TV Programme ... and calls for him to be Prime Minister.

Not another one!
BRENDA FROM BRISTOL
Reacting to Theresa May's election announcement

ZEITGEIST
Project Bubble

Escaping the Project Bubble

- ❑ Try to base yourself where you can see and hear the rest of the organisation — and you can be seen by them.

- ❑ Recruit people that get what you are doing and will promote the project with natural enthusiasm

- ❑ Get all new members of the project team to do a full induction to meet and understand how the organisation works and how it feels

- ❑ Keep communication simple and conversational.

- ❑ People rarely :
    - ☒ read blocks of text
    - ☒ open attachments to emails

- ❑ People can believe or they can be skeptical
  They will decide . . .

- ❑ Demonstrating the project team do not live in a bubble will get more complete and honest information.

- ❑ Keep message simple
    - ☒ Project people will enjoy detail but not everyone else

Finding the Zeitgeist

- ❑ Share people between the team as a job split with their own day job

- ❑ Have regular informal meetings with those involved and the project team e.g. celebration meetings for key successes, Q&A with the sponsor or project team or supplier, quiz coffee mornings

- ❑ Not understanding your audience can result in saying something that is neutral to you but will alienate some or all of your audience.

- ❑ Once found, the Zeitgeist can carry your message in a natural and believable way

> **ZEITGEIST**
> The zeitgeist of a particular place during a particular period in history is the attitudes and ideas that are generally common there at that time, especially the attitudes and ideas shown in literature, philosophy, and politics.
>
> **Collins English Dictionary**

WHAT BREXIT DID

BRITISH PUBLIC
The political elite made assumptions
REMAIN second guessed public opinion ... and misread it
- Who were they talking to ?
- Were they talking to anyone?
- Still no string clear message in 2019 Election
LEAVE use simple language
- TAKE BACK CONTROL
- GET BREXIT DONE

WESTMINSTER BUBBLE
Politicians, media and campaigners already had lifestyles that enjoyed confrontation and debate. BREXIT fuelled that and gave them more and more opportunities to enjoy the Westminster Bubble.

DIE IN A DITCH
Just before visiting Dublin, Boris Johnson said he would die in a ditch. Leading to an Irish journalist asking ... "Prime Minister when you talk about people being found 'dead in ditches' there's a sense in this country that you really don't understand what's at stake here."

ZEITGEIST
Trending

Plug into the zeitgeist

☐ Spend time asking questioning and listening to your audience

☐ Back that up by looking at evidence

- ◪ Data Data Data
  e.g. pulse surveys about how they people about the project

☐ Give your project an identity that will reflect the zeitgeist

- ◪ Find a project name that will suit the outcome and the audience — not just what the project team think is clever
  - Anacronym
  - Symbolic e.g. Voyager

- ◪ Get a good strapline or slogan
  e.g. Keeping It Simple, Driven by Data

- ◪ Decide how documents and presentations should look
  e.g. colour, typefaces, key memorable graphics

☐ Quick Wins

- ◪ What is symbolic of your change that would capture the zeitgeist?
  e.g. upgrade to new touch-screen laptops

Keep your message relevant

All through the project keep looking for what is trending with your audience.

☐ Emotions — what are they feeling happy/angry/fatigued about?

☐ Opinions — what are people talking about?

☐ Language — what words are they using?

☐ Sources — how are they getting information?

☐ What are customers talking about?

☐ How are customers talking to each other?

CONTROL THE MESSAGE
Make it easy for your influencers and the project team to repeat your messages consistently
- Simple phrases
- Relevant to the audience

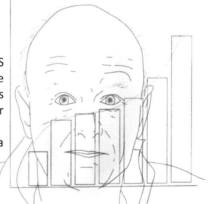

DOMINIC CUMMINGS
Analyst and advisor for the LEAVE campaign and to Boris Johnson as prime minister

Behind the data

WHAT BREXIT DID

DEMONSTRATIONS GALORE
- Extinction Rebellion
- Peoples' Vote
- Parliament Square / Green encampments
- Unparliamentary language
- Spills over to social media and onto streets
- Media conducts frenetic interviews

THE MOOD OF THE TIME
Nigel Farage
Set himself up as foil to the Westminster Bubble
£ symbolic on the logo
An Everyman performance on the campaign trail
Pushing at an open door
EMOTIVE JARGON ON RISE
- Project Fear
- Rebel Alliance
- Traitors

BREXIT ZEITGEIST
Public frustrations with politicians, civil servants, judges and media coming to a head
- Boris talks about painting buses in his spare time to google ahead of NHS bus
Reaction to tv debates/interviews/headlines misjudged by interviewers

THE SMART PLAN
Next Steps

The best practice tools and techniques featured in the book are described on many websites and in a number of great books.

Here are some of our favourites books.

THE EFFECTIVE CHANGE MANAGER'S HANDBOOK
Kogan Page (2015)
Edited by Richard Smith, David King, Ranjit Sidhu and Dan Skelsey

PROJECT MANAGING CHANGE
Prentice Hall (2009)
Ira Blake and Cindy Bush

THE CUSTOMER EXPERIENCE BOOK
Pearson (2016)
Alan Pennington

KEY BUSINESS ANALYTICS
FT Publishing (2016)
Bernard Marr

VISUAL THINKING
BISPUBLISHERS (2017)
Willemien Brand

VISUAL COLLABORATION
Wiley (2020)
Ole Qvist-Serensen and Loa Baastrup

THE WORKSHOP BOOK
Pearson (2016)
Pamela Hamilton

FUNKY BUSINESS
Pearson Education (2007)
Jonas Ridderstråle and Kjell A. Nordström

We can also provide help for your projects and ways of working.

Find out more at

www.TheSmartPlan.co.uk

Our own learning is continuous and will always remain collaborative.

Share your thoughts about the book.

www.linkedin.com/company/thesmartplan

Twitter   @plansmartly

Email   info@thesmartplan.co.uk

COMING SOON

THE SMART PLAN Workbook

The companion to this book — full of activities to support the themes we have looked at here.

Printed in Great Britain
by Amazon